Remember

Remember

{ A LITTLE BOY'S
NEAR-DEATH
Experience }

RUSSELL RICKS

CFI, an Imprint of Cedar Fort, Inc.
Springville, Utah

ISBN 13: 978-1-4621-2066-6

Published by CFI, an imprint of Cedar Fort, Inc.
2373 W. 700 S., Springville, UT 84663
Distributed by Cedar Fort, Inc., www.cedarfort.com

LIBRARY OF CONGRESS CATALOGING-IN-PUBLICATION DATA

Names: Ricks, Russell, 1958- author.
Title: Remember : a little boy's near-death experience / Russell Ricks.
Description: Springville, Utah : CFI, an imprint of Cedar Fort, Inc., [2017]
   | Includes bibliographical references and index.
Identifiers: LCCN 2017019762 (print) | LCCN 2017027003 (ebook) | ISBN
   9781462128181 (ebook) | ISBN 9781462120666 (pbk. : alk. paper)
Subjects: LCSH: Ricks, Russell, 1958- | Jesus Christ--Apparitions and
   miracles. | Jesus Christ--Knowableness. | Visions in children. | Church of
   Jesus Christ of Latter-day Saints--Doctrines. | Mormon Church--Doctrines.
   | LCGFT: Autobiographies.
Classification: LCC BX8643.J4 (ebook) | LCC BX8643.J4 R49 2017 (print) | DDC
   289.3092 [B] --dc23
LC record available at https://lccn.loc.gov/2017019762

Cover design by Shawnda T. Craig
Cover design © 2017 by Cedar Fort, Inc.
Edited and typeset by Chelsea Holdaway

Printed in the United States of America

10 9 8 7 6 5 4 3 2 1

Printed on acid-free paper

I dedicate this book to my mother, Iris Viola Hunter Ricks, who passed away September 13, 2016, at the age of eighty-two. Mom was the first person I shared my experience with over fifty years ago. I knew she would listen to me, believe me, and keep the things I shared with her in confidence.

I also dedicate this book to Dr. Elliot Sherr, director of the Brain Development Research Program at UCSF, and his research team for the benefit of helping those who suffer with callosal brain development issues.

Also on my list of professionals are Dr. Kent Gregory and Dr. Steve Osborne, who helped me in the development of management skills with my particular disabilities. A portion of the proceeds from the sale of this book will go to the Brain Development Research Program at UCSF to aid them in their important research.

And last but not least, this book is dedicated to all those who have gone through something similar, as well as those who feel socially isolated and alone in this world. You are not alone.

Praise for *Remember*

"The prophet, Joel, said: 'And it shall come to pass in the last days, saith God, I will pour out my Spirit upon all flesh: and your sons and your daughters shall prophesy, and your young men shall see visions, and your old men shall dream dreams (Acts 2:17).'

If you've ever wondered if something like this will ever happen to you, or perhaps if it already has, and you're not sure what to make of it, this work by author and artist Russell Ricks is something you will want to read. Joel was a prophet of God; he was writing the truth. Russell Ricks has learned that the veil separating this temporal world from heaven and those who reside there is thinner than most people realize."

—Lee Nelson, author of *Beyond the Veil*

———

"I dearly loved this book. It really spoke to my soul, confirming my Heavenly Father is always watching over us. It also helped me realize some of my family members might also have problems related to ACC, thus deepening my love and admiration for the trials they had to go through."

—Shawn White, SOAR (Stillwater Operation and Rescue) executive director and CEO

———

"With the sensitive eye of an artist, Ricks paints a portrait of a very special spiritual experience. His attention to the colorful wonders of his dream-vision alert us to the fact that this encounter is being reported by one who observes and appreciates the beauties of this world and the world beyond. His tender revelations about personal struggles and the healing power of God's love remind us all to be aware of the shower of blessings surrounding us as we journey down the path of life."

—Anonymous Fine Arts professional

———

"*Remember* by Russell Ricks is an interesting autobiographical book written by a practicing member of the Church of Jesus Christ of Latter-day Saints, commonly known as Mormonism.

[Ricks] is not interested in becoming famous, but exclusively wishes to share a 'very sacred' experience. His book concentrates on a largely ineffable spiritual vision or dream. The author was given this 'spiritually transformative experience' (STE) in 1966, as an eight-year-old boy, although he prefers to describes it as 'being caught up by the spirit.'

The experience includes a classical out-of-body experience and approaching a light; after which, young Ricks ends up in a small, inexpressibly beautiful garden grove, surrounded by aspen trees, flowers, and other plants. He has the strong impression he has been there before. His experience seems incredibly real, and what he perceives is more beautiful than anything he has ever laid his eyes on before. Ricks seems to have access to perfect knowledge about anything he concentrates on. It appears as if he gets to relive what happened before he descended to 'mortality'— notably the anxiety and hesitation he had felt in the process. He was comforted by someone in a long, white flowing robe whom he identifies as Jesus Christ. [He] understood that his present earthly life was going to be 'a necessary part of progression in God's plan for us.' Furthermore, the experience encompasses several spiritual lessons from Jesus, who also stresses young Ricks's great personal worth, despite the continuous bullying he was being subjected to. Jesus promises to send him messages to remind him that He loves him and has not forgotten him.

Ricks makes no secret about where he is coming from, and his LDS background is very present throughout the whole book. We can read about his Mormon relatives, ancestors, and prophets and their own visions and other spiritual experiences from the specific religious point of view of his Church. This is mostly interesting rather than irritating for readers who do not share his particular faith. The author demonstrates that his religion matches surprisingly well with his extraordinary experience, which in its turn, is clearly related to near-death experiences, even though he certainly was not literally near death when it occurred.

In my opinion, this book can be valuable to both Mormons and other readers. Within [Ricks's] vision there is a universal core message that seems to be slightly adjusted to [his] personal background. In accordance with this, he interprets much of his STE as being mostly symbolic in nature. He believes that this book is in part 'preparing the hearts of people from all walks of life, traditions, and diverse spiritual upbringings to eventually embrace all of His truths.' Readers who are not Mormons can easily interpret this as embracing the core message of his and similar experiences. Remarkably, for people who have read about children's memories of a spiritual pre-existence, the following sounds really familiar: 'I believe that each of us is born into this world with a royal heritage. We each have a plan and a purpose while we are here.' Just like many NDErs, Ricks experienced an unconditional divine love and acceptance, and a 'fulness of joy to the most exquisite and abundant degree.'

Apart from being a highly spiritual book, *Remember* is also a very personal account. We read about the author's social [struggles] and other handicaps, partly related to a physical condition known as agenesis of the corpus callosum (ACC). [We read about] the often cruel reactions to these handicaps from his peers and others, and his ensuing loneliness and lack of self-confidence. Ricks explains how shortly after his eighth birthday, this unbearable situation inspired him to ask God to take him 'home'; [and this] led to his spiritual experience.

We also read about how Ricks overcame his insecurities later in life as a professional artist, husband, and father. During [this time] he felt how the presence of God pulled him through the inner pain he [experienced]. He even describes various spiritual, miraculous, or paranormal experiences that he experienced as an adult.

This book is really unique and it deserves to be widely read."

—Titus Rivas, coauthor of *The Self Does Not Die*

"As someone who went through a modest amount of bullying growing up, I especially connected with [Russell's] story. Anyone who has had to endure the unfair stripes that come with living will feel comfort and peace. You will read about how God truly cares about us and helps us, even when we aren't aware. I am so glad I read this as it helped me be more watchful for the comfortable hugs from heaven that I can feel, but not see. I loved reading Russell's book. He tells about his experience simply; it was comfortable and unpretentious. Thank you for this book!"

—Linda Mitchell, phyical science and engineering office assistant

"If you have had a near death experience, or something similar, and wondered about it, then this book is for you. Through sharing his own spiritual experiences and his testimony, Russell Ricks wants you to know that your own experience was from God and has purpose. Russell hopes that you too may be comforted and guided by the divine compassion of the Savior and that you too may know of God's love for you, that your testimony may be strengthened."

—Marion Hamilton, retired art teacher

"Having only known Russell for a short time, I have immensely enjoyed the conversations that we have had on NDE. I am so glad that he wrote this book. It opened my eyes and my mind about being carried away in spirit. What an amazing and wonderful way to describe it. Thank you, Russell Ricks!"

—Patricia Vlietstra, friend of author

"I appreciate Russell [for] sharing his story of adversity, and the amazing experience of his youth. NDEs and similar experiences are fascinating to me. I recommend this book to anyone who wonders if there

is a God and a plan for each of our lives. This book is a testament of life beyond the veil!"
—Kathy Voeller, friend of author

———

"Russell Ricks [has] led an extraordinary life. He has written a book with a message that needs to be read by everyone. This book is well written and is outstanding. Russell Ricks is a great artist and author. He is very creative man that I am proud to call my friend."
—Scott Perry, friend of author

———

"*Remember* is beautifully scripted. The writer has a way with words and has inspiring and moving events."
—Salvador Rodriguez, friend of author

———

"Russell, thank you for your book. Thank you for opening up to me and to others. It is amazing to me how our lives are completely different, and yet similar. I know what it is like to deal with severe disabilities, the bullying, [the] fights, [being a] social outcast, [the] awkwardness, [the] loneliness, [the] depression, etc. I also know what it is like to be touched by God in a very personal and unique way. Isn't it neat how the Lord treats us all different, and yet, those differences complement each other?"
—A. Richards

Contents

Contents

Acknowledgments

Back in the summer of 2012, I felt a prompting to write down a sacred experience I had over fifty years ago. My gut said the time had come to do something with it. What that something was, I wasn't exactly sure. For me, writing this, my first book, was a labor of love. Many hours of thought and prayer have gone into the making of this book. Its development was a monumental and team effort. I would be remiss if I didn't acknowledge all those who helped make it possible.

First, I would like to thank my wife. She was my first encouragement, my open sounding board, my first editor, my best critic, and my human spell-check. She's amazing! She can spell anything, so if anything is misspelled, it's definitely not her fault!

The next person on my list I owe thanks to is my friend Lee Nelson, author of the well-known *Beyond the Veil* book series. After I approached Lee with the invitation to share my story in one of his books, he kindly read my manuscript. He then surprised me with the suggestion to write my own book, claiming I was a writer in my own right. I was humbled by his claim and very timid in my first attempts to write. Yet Lee continued to encourage me.

And a big thank-you to McKell Parsons, my nonfiction editor, and to all those who work at Cedar Fort Publishing. My apologies to anyone I may have missed.

Thanks to my many understanding NDE friends (whom I have met through the monthly meetings at Salt Lake City IANDS) for their support and encouragement.

Preface

Looking back at divers crossroads in my life, I have witnessed the hand of God pointing directly to the fulfillment of experiences and promises that were made to me in a miraculous event I had as a small boy. After nearly five decades, I now feel a powerful prompting to share what happened to me with the world. Some have criticized me for sharing something so personal and so sacred, yet I have come to realize that there are others who could benefit from hearing my story. Those who have gone through something similar need to know that they are not crazy and that their own experience is valid.

The Near Death Experience (or NDE)—a phrase most often used to refer to accounts of clinical death, breaching the veil of heaven, then returning to life—was coined by Dr. Raymond Moody in the 1970s. The NDE has since become a household term. Giving credit again to Dr. Moody, the NDE is now widely embraced by general society among many nations. In the United States alone, it is currently estimated that more than eighteen million of its citizens have had an NDE or similar experience.[1] Extensive research studies have been done since Dr. Moody wrote his first book on the subject, *Life After Life.*

---

1 "How Many NDEs Occur in the United States Every Day?," Jeffrey Long, *NDERF*, accessed April 27, 2017, www.nderf.org/NDERF/Research /number_nde_usa.htm. See also George Gallup Jr. and William Proctor, *Adventures in Immortality* (McGraw-Hill Book Company, 1982).

Because of revelations given to Joseph Smith Jr., the founder of the Church of Jesus Christ of Latter-day Saints (LDS), and other modern-day LDS prophets, the LDS Church has added information to its official doctrine regarding life after death, as well as the Church's doctrine of where we came from before we were born into mortality. This knowledge of an individual's existence beyond the veil has been part of the Church's doctrine since its founding in 1830. This doctrine is referred to as the plan of salvation or the great plan of happiness.

Today, some scientists are beginning to rethink the established scientific theory of the origin of the universe; more and more new evidence points to the intelligent design of the world we live in. Even some well-known, self-declared atheists and agnostic scientists are beginning to publicly admit that the evidence of an intelligent creator is strong,[2] saying it is much easier to prove intelligent design by some higher being than to attempt to prove otherwise.

In the field of NDE research today, researchers have developed a list of classic similarities that an NDE must possess in order to qualify as authentic. The following characteristics are common in NDEs: feeling intense emotions, having an out-of-body experience, moving from darkness to light, being "somewhere else," experiencing rapid observations, meeting with loved ones or sacred figures, and reliving past actions.[3] Researchers have currently classified what happened to me as a Spiritually Transformative Experience (STE).[4] My experience can also be considered an NDLE (near-death-like experience). Interesting enough, what I experienced was very similar to a classic NDE in nearly every detail. For decades, I've wondered *why*? I believe there is a scriptural definition

---

2   Casey Luskin, "Does Intelligent Design Help Science Generate New Knowledge?," *Evolution News & Science Today*, November 23, 2010, www.evolutionnews.org/2010/11/does_intelligent_design_help_s/.

3   "Characteristics of a Near-Death Experience," IANDS, accessed April 27, 2017, iands.org/ndes/about-ndes/characteristics.html.

4   See "Russell R Experience," Russell Ricks, *OBERF.org*, accessed April 27, 2017, www.oberf.org/russell_r_ste.htm.

for what the modern man calls a near-death experience. Throughout the Bible, this event is referred to as being "~~caught up by the Spirit,~~" "~~caught away,~~" or "~~carried away.~~"⁵ In trying to understand my experience better, I believe being "caught up" seems to describe what occurred in my case. ~~Even still, *how* it happened (though my curiosity drives me to want to know) is less important than *why* it happened.~~

Before I share the actual experience with you, I want you to understand that this was very real and is very sacred to me. I do not share it lightly. I seek no public notoriety. At the same time, what happened to me was so profound that I wish I could tell everyone and have them changed because of it. If I seek any reward, it would be for the Spirit of the Lord to accompany my thoughts and words so the readers will be edified and comforted.

Unfortunately, I realize not everyone will receive my experience in the way I would hope. In spite of those who are skeptical by nature, I believe there are those who would benefit from my words. Perhaps my experience will comfort them, like I was comforted by the divine compassion of the Savior. Even to this day, I am comforted by His compassion. Now, fifty plus years later, I continue to find great comfort in the love and compassion the Savior gave me during my precious time across the veil. If my simple words can help lift someone's soul and increase their faith, or even begin to change just one individual child of God, I feel like the purpose in my sharing was accomplished.

Not long after this remarkable event, I went on a personal quest to find out if anyone else had experienced something similar. I found the book *Life Everlasting* by Duane S. Crowther to be particularly comforting. The first edition of this book was introduced in 1967, about one year after a most miraculous event in my life. Around a decade later, I discovered the accounts of many others who had a Near Death Experience.

---

5   In the Old Testament, see 2 Corinthians 12:2, 4. In the New Testament, see Acts 8:39; Revelation 21:10; Revelation 17:3. In the Book of Mormon, see 1 Nephi 11:1, 19; 3 Nephi 28:13. In the Pearl of Great Price, see Moses 6:64 and Moses 7:27.

That's when I began to realize that many of the common aspects from one NDE to another were surprisingly similar to my own experience. "How was this possible," I puzzled, "unless it really did come from God?"

The experience that happened to me was very real. There was no question about that in my mind. My NDLE brought me great spiritual and emotional comfort. I cannot speak for my church—the Church of Jesus Christ of Latter-day Saints—since I am only a lay member of my faith and do not have any position of authority to claim what I witnessed as official Church doctrine, nor will I claim that what I witnessed is exactly how the kingdom of heaven is. I would never make such a claim. I will leave that up to the Lord and His appointed servants. I can only relate the event the best I know how, using the language I have been given, though it may be inadequate.

I do believe that much of what I saw was more symbolic than literal—for the purpose of teaching divine truths. In the scriptures, the Lord teaches us by using the pattern of type and symbol. I believe this experience was shown to me in a way that I could more clearly embrace and understand. I tend to be very visual and connect more easily with visually symbolic concepts. Writing this account is a first for me. As an artist, I'm more comfortable with a brush in my hand than a pen. It will be very difficult for me to paint with words, but I'll try my best. Not only is writing a book a challenging endeavor for me, the event itself was really indescribable. Nevertheless, I will do my best.

Originally, when I began sharing many of the details of my experience with others, I found that some appreciated what I shared, respecting its sacredness, and others were less impressed, even mocking me. Some, acting angry or fearful of my experience, gave me that "Have you flipped your lid? Do you have a screw loose?" eye-roll look. This really shocked me because some of these people were individuals I considered to be close confidants. Since then, and learning from past negative experiences, I've tried not to share this experience with others unless I felt prompted to do so.

So why am I writing this book after so many years of mostly public silence?

Acting upon a recent prompting of the Spirit, I decided that the time has come to put it in writing. Near-death experiences have gained popularity and have become more widely accepted today. Many people have heard of NDE research and are now more open to the concept. There seems to be a spiritual awakening; the Lord is hastening His work inside and outside of His restored Church. Surely the Lord is *pouring out His Spirit upon all flesh* (see Joel 2:28; Acts 2:17). I believe that at least part of the Lord's work is in preparing the hearts of people from all walks of life, traditions, and diverse spiritual upbringings to eventually embrace all of His truths.

More and more people from diverse backgrounds and from every nation (Christian and non-Christian) are connecting with truth and are having experiences similar to mine. I believe that the Spirit of the Lord is truly being "pour[ed] out . . . upon all flesh" (see Joel 2:28; Acts 2:17) to prepare their hearts to eventually receive the Lord's message of salvation.

> And it shall come to pass afterward, that I will pour out my spirit upon all flesh; and your sons and your daughters shall prophesy, your old men shall dream dreams, your young men shall see visions. (Joel 2:28)

I believe our lives existed before we were born into mortality and that we will continue as immortalized beings after we die. The concept and reality of the premortal existence of our spirits has been taught since the dawn of man. We existed before our mortal birth as literal spirit children of our Heavenly Father, with distinct personality traits. Even though the doctrine of a premortal existence was discarded as heretic teaching at Nicaea in AD 325, this did not change the truth. A handful of important early Christian scholars continued to believe and preach the doctrine of premortal life.

There are at least three basic reasons I feel compelled to share my experience.

1. I wish that everyone could know and feel for themselves the amazing and incredible love God has for each of us individually.

2. After keeping my experience mostly to myself for so many years, the Spirit of the Lord has moved upon me to do more with it. The process of writing and researching has helped me to assimilate and digest my personal experience, helping me to begin to understand what exactly happened and why. I also believe God is hastening His work and wants all to know of His love for them. It seems that God is quietly preparing the hearts of those who are searching for real answers to receive God's truths. There also appears to be a new age of great spiritual awakening in our day. Is this in preparation for something far more glorious in our future?

3. The Latter-day Saint prophet Joseph Smith, Jr. said we should all earnestly work to gain a knowledge of the world of spirits, so why should we fear this important subject?

All men know that they must die. And it is important that we should understand . . . our departure hence. . . . It is but reasonable to suppose that God would reveal something in reference to the matter, and it is a subject we ought to study more than any other. We ought to study it day and night, for the world is ignorant in reference to their true condition and relation. If we have any claim on our Heavenly Father for anything, it is for knowledge on this important subject.[6]

The story I am about to share—my story—is about witnessing a window of my life before I was born. It is also about my social struggles with my peers—being abused, teased, picked on, beat up, and bullied. It is about living with, learning about, and overcoming the trials and challenges of having two disabilities, and not having real friends.

My story includes getting married and raising a family of seven children, followed by a painful divorce, and finally, charting a new course, which led to marrying my soul mate of now seventeen plus years. Like

6 Joseph Smith, in *History of the Church*, 6:50.

the Old Testament prophet Job, this new course led to double the blessings of a new companion, double the children, and many grandchildren.

Through it all, and because of a miraculous event in my life, I came to truly know that I wasn't alone after all. I came to understand, to know, and to truly feel the incredible unconditional love and personal companionship of my Savior, and my dearest friend, Jesus Christ. God is very aware of each of us; He loves us, knows us personally, and is very in tune with what we need.

CHAPTER I
Curious Memories

What's your earliest memory? How young were you when you had this memory?

When I was a teenager, I once told my dad that I remembered a time as an infant when I bumped my head on the glove compartment of our family car while mom was holding me in her arms. My father was quite surprised that I had retained this memory because he said I was only about six months old when it happened.

Dad told me that, at that time, the family had decided to take a one-week vacation down south to New Mexico. I was born on July 15, 1958, in Rexburg, Idaho. This would place our holiday vacation early in the year of 1959, around January. While on a mountain pass, a nearby car had veered into our lane as it sped around a curve, forcing Dad to hit the brakes hard. No one was seriously hurt, but I must have hit my head hard enough that I could remember how bad it hurt!

According to a 2014 *Scientific American* magazine article, "What's Your First Memory?" research hints that infants zero to two years old *can* form brief memories.[1] Newborns seem to immediately identify their parents' voices, specifically their mother's voice, only moments after they

---

1 Victoria Stern, "What's Your First Memory," *Scientific American*, September 1, 2014, www.scientificamerican.com/article/what-s-your-first-memory/.

are born.[2] Are we born with the memory of our parents' voices because we already learned to identify the sound of their voice while still in the womb? I think there is some truth to this.

Parents often report that their infant stares off into space, or smiles and laughs as if someone is standing before their eyes, yet to the parents, there appears to be no one there. Could we, as parents, be mistaken? Do infants see angels, or perhaps the spirits of their progenitors? Since infants have recently come from heaven, do they retain a memory of the premortal heavenly realm? I believe this is possible, and I will tell you why.

———

My mother was blessed with the gift of singing. She had the most beautiful, professionally trained, high soprano voice, and I always thought she sang like an angel.

In the summer of 1946, when my mother was sixteen, she visited her Uncle Ralph and Aunt Devota in Seattle for the summer. While she was there, Mom entered a talent contest, winning second place in the competition. Backstage, Mom was approached by a talent scout from the United Service Organization (USO), whose purpose was to find fresh talent to entertain the military servicemen in the Northwest. Singing with the USO, she became one of the most favored entertainers, getting frequent encores to come back onstage for one last number.

The summer of 1949, Mom went to Hollywood and auditioned before Mr. Gordon, an employee of Warner Brothers Studios. She got an offer to work as a regular movie extra through Warner Bros., and to work as a maid for Gordon's family in exchange for vocal lessons.

Gordon had an ongoing contract with Warner Brothers Studios to teach actors and actresses how to sing. In my mother's own words, "It was as good an offer as any, for anyone in my situation to get into show biz."

---

2   Laura Flynn Mccarthy, "What Babies Learn in the Womb," *Parenting*, accessed April 27, 2017, www.parenting.com/article/what-babies-learn-in -the-womb.

Gordon warned her about the total commitment a singing and acting career would require and how she would have to set aside any thoughts of putting a family first. Her family would have to come second. A few days later, Mom told Gordon that she would have to turn down his offer, because raising a family of her own and having a happy marriage was what she truly wanted out of life. Even still, Mom was so talented with her voice; she had a pretty good shot at becoming a famous actress if she wanted. I'm glad she chose family.

As an infant, I remember being held in her arms or cradled on her hip while she sang a variety of popular melodies. As a toddler, one song, "Beautiful Blue Eyes," made me very jealous of my blue-eyed younger brother, Marty. After Marty was born, I felt like I had lost what I thought was my rightful place in my mother's arms. By the time I could talk a little, I would jealously beg my mother to sing a song about brown eyes so she would hold me too. Mom would try to accommodate by changing the words to "Beautiful Brown Eyes."

My mother's name was Iris Viola Hunter Ricks. She was eighty-two when she passed away on September 13, 2016, just four days shy of her eighty-third birthday.

I shared the following experience of an early memory with my mother about eight months prior to her passing. She was visibly touched by what I told her after keeping it to myself for over five decades. For Mom, I think it helped put into perspective the impact her singing had on all people.

A day hardly ever went by without Mom singing something. This memory of my mother making music goes back to a time before I had the skill to form my thoughts into words. It is a very precious and curious memory to my mind. I was older than six months and younger than two years. I remember feeling frustrated that I couldn't express things that I felt were important for my family to hear from me.

It seemed that every time Mom would sing or play the piano, my siblings and I were not the only ones who enjoyed Mom's entertainment.

Remember

I have memories of elderly looking men and women dressed in white entering our home often and sitting near my mother while she sang. These personages had forms like a physical body, except they appeared somewhat transparent. I observed that sometimes they would sit quietly and listen and sometimes they sang by her side. Mom's angelic voice was so beautiful, it seemed to literally attract angels from beyond the veil. I wanted to ask everyone who these people were, and I tried to communicate it, but apparently, no one would listen to me or could see what I could see. It appeared that I was the only one who noticed they were there. My attempt to get their attention seemed almost humorous. I remember thinking how strange this was. Now that my mother has moved on to the world of spirits, I sometimes like to think she has joined an angelic choir.

Recently, I shared this memory with my wife, Karen. My wife is an expert in genealogy research. She suggested we Google my mother's ancestors. My mom's parents were William Wallace Hunter and Bertha O'Donnell Hunter. I specifically remember the likeness of one of the elderly men. He wore glasses and had a full head of thick, white hair. On my Grandma Hunter's side, we found a picture of an uncle of hers who I thought resembled this man in my memory, except he appeared to be much older when I saw him than he was in the photo available online. Of course, I have no way of proving this memory, but I personally believe the veil between heaven and earth is very thin, and that these visitors were the spirits of my mother's deceased ancestors.

Can infants see angels? LDS scripture tells us that we were first created as literal spirit children of a loving Father in Heaven before we came to earth (see Moses 3:5, 7). We came from heaven to fulfill a special purpose while in mortality. We live on as intelligent, individual, and spiritual beings after our physical body is placed in the grave.

I believe in the possibility that when we are first born into this world, we come with some fresh memories from our premortal past. I also believe that after we die, we are still very much involved with and responsible for our posterity, even as my deceased grandfather communicated his concern for his posterity (see Appendix). ~~Perhaps we ourselves even become some of our children's guardian or auxiliary angels after we die.~~

One day at work, my sister Becky sent me a text: she didn't want to be alone when Mom died. Before I arrived, Becky said that Mom's breathing was fairly normal. By the time I arrived and walked into Mom's room, her breathing had become more labored and continued to decline. She did not appear conscious. It became clear that her body was breaking down; her organs were shutting down one by one.

When I had paid Mom a visit the weekend previous, she told me she was afraid to die. I was heartbroken when I heard her express this and did my best to comfort her. She had been an inactive member of the Church of Jesus Christ of Latter-day Saints for over twenty years. Mom played a huge role in building the character and moral development of our family. Mom had always been the person I could talk to about anything without feeling criticism or judgment. During my visit, I reminded her of the morning back in 1966 when I had crossed the veil. I reminded her that she was the very first person I shared the experience with because I trusted her confidentiality and approachable nature.

Mom nodded and smiled. "Yes, I do remember!"

My mother had brought the gift of life, comfort, and love to me on so many occasions. Now it was my turn to return her precious gift.

"Mom, you have nothing to be afraid of. Look back on your life and the way you raised us and loved us. There is nothing to be ashamed of. No other woman but you could have been a better mother to her children or a wife to her husband!"

A few more comforting words and moments were shared before I had to leave for work.

When I returned to her bedside a few days later, Mom smiled brightly when she saw me enter the room.

"Hi, Russell," she beamed, looking and pointing upward.

"Mom, are you no longer afraid?"

She shook her head "no." She was smiling widely, and her happy face seemed aglow with heaven's light.

Had someone from across the veil visited my mother? I thought to myself. During this visit with her, there were other precious things that happened and seemed to indicate that she had previously had visitors from the other side. One of those instances was when she called out to her mother (my Grandma Hunter) several times while I was there.

It was not long after when my sister sent me a text asking that I stay with her during Mom's final moments. A short while after I came, Becky invited me to take her place by Mom's side. As I did so, I caressed her precious face and held her withered hand. After a time, I began to sense a strong presence of others in the room with us. To my eyesight, there was no one there except Mom, Becky, and I, yet I had the sense that our deceased father and my mother's parents had joined us. They came to comfort and escort their dear one home. It was not just a premonition that they had come, but there was a powerful feeling of warmth and comfort that enveloped the room. The Spirit communicated with me and bore witness that they were there. This feeling continued for several hours, although I didn't see them with my natural eyes. Perhaps you could call it a Shared Death Experience (SDE), but only in the sense that I felt the presence of close family from across the veil. I did witness a brief confirmation of these visitors at the very moment she took her final breath. In the early hours of Tuesday morning, on September 13, at 2:49 a.m., her time finally came. To my surprise, Mom briefly opened her eyes, first looking at me, then briskly looking to her left and up. She gasped with joyful surprise and her body shrank. She dropped her head and slipped away. She was gone. At that moment, the feeling I had of those who came to escort her home left the room with her.

I believe our deceased ancestors are very aware of our doings and are watching over us. The following chapter shows that perhaps I had a few of my own keeping watch over me.

CHAPTER 2
Growing Up at Home

When I was of age to attend kindergarten, my parents decided to keep me home. They recognized that I was not ready; whenever they brought up the subject of going to school soon, I would throw a tantrum. I wanted to stay home and play with my younger brother, Marty. I am certain my parents were looking forward to the brief break it would give them during the day, so they could get some relief from my childhood antics. Here are some examples of those experiences.

When I was around two years old, my mother went into the bathroom to fill the bathtub with water so she could get ready to go somewhere. While the tub was filling, she let herself get distracted and left the bathroom for what she first intended to be a brief moment.

Apparently, getting temporarily sidetracked and forgetting she was in the middle of filling the bathtub, she was suddenly brought to her senses with an image in her mind of me floating in the water facedown. She dropped whatever she was doing, ran upstairs, down the hall, and into the bathroom, just as I was leaning over the side of the tub and lifting a leg to get in.

Another example is the following story. The home I grew up in had a large front yard, which made it a long walk out to the mailbox near the street. One summer afternoon, at the age of about five, I followed my mother on her usual routine out to the mailbox. With my short little legs, I followed Mom a few paces behind her. She was unaware of my presence (Mom was hard of hearing in one ear). She stepped out to the curb and stuck her hand in the mailbox.

At the same moment, a semitruck was quickly coming up the road toward us. I jumped out in the street in front of the semi, holding my hands out, palms forward, my arms stretched out in front of me. I had a big confident grin on my face and playfully bellowed, "Look, Mom, watch this!"

The frightened driver behind the wheel of the truck slammed on his brakes, coming to a sudden stop only a few inches away from my outstretched arms. The driver then stepped out to see if everything was all right. His face looked white and his eyes were as big as dinner plates. He was visibly shaken.

He was relieved, seeing that I was unharmed and grinning, with my arms still outstretched. He said, "I didn't see anything, but something told me to stop immediately!" Still unnerved, he apologized to my mom, climbed back into his truck, and drove away. What was my little mind thinking? Certainly, the angels in heaven had to do double duty with me, just to keep me alive!

Another story, about the same time period, involved my bedroom window on the second floor of our house, roughly twenty feet above ground level. Several feet below the window (on the ground level), stood a large exterior coal bin. One day, I jumped out of the window, attempting to fly, and landed barefoot in the coal bin below. Delighted and unharmed, I ran back into the house, up the stairs to my room, and did it again and again and again.

———

But eventually, when school started up in the fall, shortly after I turned seven, Mom dragged me, kicking and screaming, to school. I did everything I could think of to avoid attending. Being surrounded by dozens of individuals I didn't know and being teased and taunted by unkind peers filled me with anxiety and fear. For that reason, school terrified me! Up to this point in my life, experience had shown me that I couldn't trust the world outside the security of my own home.

CHAPTER 3
Peer Troubles

I didn't enjoy school. If I did manage to make a friend, they were most often a misfit or an outcast. Because of all of this, I had low self-esteem and a low self-image.

It wasn't long after the school year started that my worst fears were confirmed. During recess, no one wanted to play games with me. It didn't matter what games we played, no one wanted me on their team, and they would openly vocalize this. I was *always* the last one picked.

Even my first-grade teacher, Mrs. Cook, terrified me. In my mind, she was the perfect duplicate of the Wicked Witch of the West in *The Wizard of Oz*!

Back in those days (the mid-1960s), the old-school method of disciplining disobedient students often included getting whipped with a willow switch or a stick. Mrs. Cook would sometimes literally break wooden yardsticks over my head, back, or hands.

Nowadays, teachers could easily lose their jobs or go to jail for doing such things. I am so glad this kind of behavior is so carefully watched these days. Little children are tender and undeserving of such abusive behavior. They need to be treated with love and should be able to trust without fear.

Thankfully, Mrs. Cook retired a few years later, but not until after inflicting her harsh disciplinary nature upon other tender souls. No doubt, they would later have their own troubling stories to tell. Here are some examples of how Mrs. Cook dealt with me.

Mrs. Cook would often embarrass me in front of the entire class, which only added to the abuse I suffered from my peers during recess. One example occurred when I scribbled out my errors and smudged my paper instead of using an eraser, because I couldn't find an eraser in my desk.

The inside of my desk was very cluttered. Mrs. Cook complained about the messy paper and my scribbles. (I am left-handed and therefore had difficulty not making smudges.) When I told her I couldn't find my eraser, she stormed over and jerked open my desk. Seeing the mess only flared her anger more, so she dug out all my belongings like a dog and let them fall to the floor. *Whack, whack, whack* went the yardstick over my left wrist. Then she made me pick it all up. All my peers were laughing at me. Things like this only gave my classmates more fuel to tease and torment me.

I am certain that Mrs. Cook's abusive behavior contributed to the emotional and physical beatings I suffered almost daily from my classmates. After school, these bullies would gang up on me, beating me up for entertainment.

I couldn't understand why I was being treated this way. I only wanted to be their friend. In my mind, I tried to be nice to everyone, but I guess I was an easy target. When I would react to their teasing and taunting, they only wanted to ridicule me more.

It wasn't until many years later that I was able to understand why I was so easy to tease. This realization didn't come until I was fifty. For my age (even after I became an adult), my social skills were behind and underdeveloped. How to socially interact and get along well with my peers was far beyond my comprehension. I will discuss this later in my story.

For much of my life, I was pretty much a loner and was quite reclusive. It was a miracle I survived, and it was likely because of a specific miracle that I managed to get through all those years. This miracle happened to me during my childhood and is the reason I was prompted to write my story. But first, let's get back to my school years.

Another memory I have of my first-grade teacher shows my stubbornness, defiance, and contrary nature developed in my early years. I am certain this part of my personality came about as a defense mechanism, in an effort to protect what I still held onto proudly as my own identity.

One day, I was asked to come up to the chalkboard at the front of the class to draw a big capital letter "A." I felt this was a subject I knew something about; it was my chance to prove to the class and to Mrs. Cook that I was not stupid.

Mrs. Cook had marked three horizontal dotted lines on the board—one set of lines at the top, one set in the middle, and one set at the bottom—indicating where we were to write a given letter form. I was handed some chalk and began at the bottom left, drawing the diagonal line up to the right until I met the top dotted line. I was about to go to the bottom right and make the second diagonal line, but the next thing I knew, my hands were being whacked with a wooden yardstick. Mrs. Cook then said that I was not doing it the way it was supposed to be done; I was supposed to start at the top, drawing the line downward.

I stubbornly told her, "You're wrong! My dad is a professional sign-painter and he knows what he is doing. He starts at the bottom, painting his letters upward, and his letters are all perfect!"

She was also angry because I used my left hand to write, and when she tried to get me to switch I said, "This is my *right* hand, because I *write* with it!" Mrs. Cook then broke the yardstick in half over my head. I was laughed at and was again embarrassed in front of the class.

—

I later learned the main reason my dad formed his painted letters from the bottom upward was to prevent the paint from running or dripping down the handle of the lettering brush. In my early adult years, I also became a sign painter and could paint a block-styled letter to near perfection. (Not too bad for a lefty, eh?) My dad said my hand-lettered block-lettering skills were better than his.

——

When the end of my first-grade school year came around, I could not wait for summer to begin, and I'm sure I was the happiest kid alive! I felt relieved, at least for a three-month break, from suffering the daily and ever-constant abuse of my teacher and classmates. The end of my first-grade year was 1966, and I would turn eight in the upcoming July.

My first school experience was so abusive and miserable for me, it was no wonder I didn't look forward to the following school year, but I knew I had no choice.

Fortunately, when I did return to Kennedy Elementary for second grade, I got some relief. Mrs. Fern Ricks, a distant relative of my family, was very patient and kind. She was my favorite teacher, and I still think about her often with gratitude in my heart.

She recognized my social immaturity when compared to my peers, but she gave me the space I needed to be who I was. She also told my parents, "Even though Russell often places behind his peers in his school assignments, he is very smart. Once he gets it, he gets it, and he never forgets it!" That was a very kind thing for her to say. I must say that I really loved her for being so very kind and patient with me.

I really felt she loved me. By the end of the school year, Mrs. Ricks suggested to my parents that I be held back one more year. At first I objected, worrying that this would give my peers more ammunition to taunt and tease me with. Unfortunately, it turned out to be an accurate assumption.

But when my mom told me that I would be in Mrs. Ricks's class again, I finally agreed to it. I looked to Mrs. Ricks as my angel and rescuer from the hurt I felt from those around me. She had such a joyful, gentle, and loving demeanor; she was always so kind to me.

——

The teasing and abuse from many of my peers continued at a fever pitch, up to about ninth grade. One afternoon, during Mr. Stowell's symphony band class, I must have somehow made a classmate angry. A kid shorter than me said he was going to beat me up after school.

I never wanted to pick a fight with anyone, yet here it was happening again. I figured the fight would be a piece of cake, since this kid was shorter than me and appeared kind of scrawny. After school, I just wanted to get it over with and go home, so I waited outside at the agreed place behind the junior high. When I got there, I waited alone for about ten minutes.

A few minutes later, this little kid showed up, along with the school bully. I became really angry and quite afraid that I was not going to win the fight. I found out that, on account of the size of the kid who was mad at me, the school bully would take his place.

I knew I wouldn't be able to back out of the situation, so I took courage and determined that if I got out of it alive, at least I would prove to myself that I wasn't a coward.

When the fight began, I didn't get in the first punch or land very many punches afterward, for that matter. I pretty much became a punching bag and was severely beaten.

After a few minutes, my eyes, cheekbones, jaw, and mouth were bloodied and swollen. My body was bruised pretty much from head to foot. Even though I was losing, I was so mad that the little punk got someone else to fight his battles for him that I was determined not to quit.

I wasn't going to win, but I resolved to die trying. I knew that heaven would be a much happier place anyway; I was tired of having to face this life without any real friends. In heaven, I knew without a doubt that I had a true friend in Christ. I wasn't going to let anyone call me a coward, or make fun of me ever again. If I did die, I knew life would be much better on the other side of the veil.

Finally, the bully saw how bad I was getting clobbered, and I think it finally got to him. He cried out, "Say Uncle!"

I angrily shot back, "No, this is an unfair fight! I won't let anyone call me a coward and the whole school will know I stood up to you!"

Again the bully repeated, "Say Uncle!"

"No!" I screamed.

The bully punched me a few more times and finally said, "I've had enough!" then turned and walked away.

The following school day, there was a rumor going around school that I had stood up to the bully and won the fight. From that day forward, my peers pretty much left me alone and treated me with greater respect, though I still had no real friends.

———

It was not until well into adulthood (around age fifty) that I understood the cause of my frequent social challenges. I learned through an MRI scan of my brain that I was born with a rare neurological disorder called agenesis of the corpus callosum (ACC). ACC is a condition where "the corpus callosum is absent."[1] The corpus callosum is the "largest midline structure of the brain." It connects the two hemispheres in the brain and transfers motor, sensory, and cognitive information between the hemispheres.[2] In my case, I had complete agenesis (cACC), or in other words, the corpus callosum appeared to be completely missing from my brain. This disability resulted in my having a severe social delay. Sometimes, I was later mislabeled as having some other type of clinical behavioral issue, like ADHD.

Living with ACC throughout my life has not been easy. Clearly understanding social nuances as well as correctly reading the body

———

1   "What Is Agenesis of the Corpus Callosum (ACC)?," College of Education and Human Development, *University of Maine*, accessed May 1, 2017, umaine.edu/edhd/research/acc/what-is-agenesis-of-the-corpus-callosum -acc/. See also "Corpus Callosum Disorders," *National Organization for Disorders of the Corpus Callosum*, accessed May 1, 2017, nodcc.org/corpus -callosum-disorders/#cc.

2   Ibid.

language of others has been extremely challenging. Before realizing my disability, I had also developed incorrect habits of communicating.

On top of that, I was born with nerve damage in my left ear, which led to severe hearing loss that has now progressed to both ears. These two disabilities have contributed to monumentally challenging communication and social roadblocks. Eventually, I was able to get help from some very good therapists. My wife, Karen, has also been amazing with her loving support.

It was both a shock and a relief when Karen and I finally understood why I struggled so much with communication and social things. It was a shock to learn about this rare disorder, and we marveled at the fact that I can even function at all, even though the corpus callosum part of my brain is completely nonexistent! Somehow, my brain rerouted itself during its early stages of development in the womb, allowing me to now function at a fairly normal level in society—though not completely normal. It was also a relief to better understand what has been the root cause of my challenges.

———

I knew both of my parents loved me. I was never physically abused or harshly disciplined by either of them. Yet due to life's stresses and adversities, my father would often be gruff in the way he spoke to me.

Feeling insecure about myself, I would demand his attention to the point of annoying him.

If Dad did get upset with me, or one of my siblings, he had a saying he used to get us to "straighten up." He'd say, "Knock it off or I'll get out the old frozen boot!" We never actually saw the "frozen boot," yet we all did what he asked.

After years of dealing with many of life's stresses and frustrations, Dad had developed a permanent crease in his brow that we called "the mad eyebrows." Most of the time, all Dad had to do was look at us with those "mad eyebrows" and threaten the "frozen boot." That always worked! My siblings and I now each have a memorial to Dad's "frozen boot" hanging in our homes that one of my sisters made as a Christmas gift.

During my teen years, I rarely got along with my dad. I tried several times, without success, to get him to apologize for past unkind acts he'd done to me. A vocal apology was never his way. It wasn't until a few months before Dad passed away at the age of sixty-six that I actually heard a verbal apology from him, and, for the first time, saw him cry.

Underneath that gruff, macho facade was an insecure but tender-hearted man. Dad was not one to show his emotions publicly. I had already resolved his past unkind acts in my own mind, and had privately forgiven him years before, but it was good to hear him vocally ask for my forgiveness and help me to heal further.

———

Although most of the abuse I suffered came to an end after high school, I still continued to struggle socially throughout adulthood. Through it all, I turned to oil painting as an escape from all the social rejection I felt. I also felt the presence of God in my life pull me through my inner pain.

You might be asking yourself at this point, "With two severe disabilities, how did Russell manage to survive the first fifty years of his life?" Well, it hasn't been easy.

Though it has often left me feeling lonely, I came to understand, to feel, and to *know* that I wasn't really alone. During the difficult times, I often reflected on an extraordinary event that happened to me shortly after my eighth birthday. I came to know for myself that God is real, that He truly does love me, that He is my friend, and that He is very aware of my existence. How did I come by this knowledge? My journey began many years ago.

CHAPTER 4
No Tongue Can Speak

On one precious summer night, between my first and second year in grade school, a miraculous event happened in my life that I have never forgotten. I still remember the details vividly to this day (more than fifty years later) of when I was taken to the other side of this mortal veil, into the world of spirits.

—

When I was only eight years old, the Lord answered my earnest and tearful plea in a miraculous way. Heavenly Father knows each of us individually, and He knows us so well that His abundant tender mercies are intricately tailored to us specifically. His tender mercies can bring us great comfort and peace. The answer I sought came with great abundance and hit me very powerfully. It was exactly what I needed, but it didn't come in the way I would have expected. The truth is, how do you share an experience that was so overwhelming, so moving, so life-changing, and so incredible that there are not adequate words in the human language to fully express it?

In heaven, there is so much love, purity, perfection, and truth displayed on such diverse levels and spectrums that the best words in the human language could not even begin to scratch the surface.

For example, consider the words of an ancient American prophet named Nephi who also struggled forming the right words to express a sacred event when his people were visited by the resurrected Lord and Savior Jesus Christ, shortly after He hung on the cross in Jerusalem:

And after this manner do they bear record: The eye hath never seen, neither hath the ear heard, before, so great and marvelous things as we saw and heard Jesus speak unto the Father;

And no tongue can speak, neither can there be written by any man, neither can the hearts of men conceive so great and marvelous things as we both saw and heard Jesus speak; and no one can conceive of the joy which filled our souls at the time we heard him pray for us unto the Father.

And it came to pass that when Jesus had made an end of praying unto the Father, he arose; but so great was the joy of the multitude that they were overcome. (3 Nephi 17:16–18)

So great were the Savior's words to the Nephites and the Lamanites who witnessed this miraculous event that no man had the power to express, or even attempt to, write His words.

If there is a single phrase that can at least somewhat express this ineffable feeling, and using the language I do have the power to express, it would be to experience a *fulness of joy to the most exquisite and abundant degree*. Still, for what happened to me and to thousands of others, man cannot completely and adequately form the words. So great was the power of this experience, it is truly beyond description. With this in mind, I will now do my best to describe what to me was a reality.

CHAPTER 5

Young Men Shall Dream Dreams

I was baptized at the young age of eight years old into The Church of Jesus Christ of Latter-day Saints. A few weeks after I became a member of the Church, I remember feeling how wonderful it was to have my slate wiped clean.

At that time in my life, I was pure! I remember thinking that if I just stayed in bed and didn't have to get up and face the trials and temptations of the day, I could keep myself unspotted. I was also afraid to face my peers, for fear of being a target of continual teasing, beatings, and bullying. Life outside the protection of my home was so traumatic and threatening. I didn't want to go back to such a miserable, scary experience. I believed heaven was a place where I would feel safe and loved. I so wanted to leave this existence and go back home to heaven. With those thoughts in my mind, I prayed earnestly with the Lord to take me home if it was His will.

After my prayer, I climbed into the comfort of my bed and then tearfully drifted off to sleep feeling depressed, frightened, and unloved. As I began to fall asleep, I felt the common sensation of the bed slowly spinning. As it spun, it seemed my body, or perhaps my spirit (I'm not sure which), rose up from my spinning bed and continued to ascend upward into the darkness of the night.

Russell Ricks, *Place of Refuge*, oil on canvas, 14 in. × 11 in.
Painted from memory, in an attempt to capture an
impression of the aspen grove from Russell's NDLE.

After a time, I sensed a tiny beam of light in the distance above me. As I drew closer to the light, it expanded and continued to increase in brightness until it filled the entirety of the space around me. Next, I found myself standing high on a mountainside, in the midst of a small, inexpressibly beautiful garden grove. I was surrounded by what appeared to be aspen trees, a variety of flowers, and other pleasant forest plant life. Some of the flowers looked familiar, and some were of a variety I had never seen before, with variations of colors I had never laid my eyes upon.

Despite the unfamiliarity, I had a strong sensation of déjà vu in this space. The trees and the plant life on the forest floor were similar to what we might find on earth, but were far more glorious and otherworldly.

Though familiar in that sense, I quickly perceived that the place where I stood was not anywhere on earth. It was sacred, holy ground in some sort of spiritual realm. Along with that simple observation, everything seemed so incredibly real that, when I started to research what had happened to me, I was unsure at first whether I was having an actual near-death-like experience or if I was having a dream—a vision if you will. In fact, the whole experience seemed more vibrant and real than the reality we experience here on earth.

(Later in my life, I discovered that what experts call an NDE was remarkably parallel to my experience, in terms of the classic similarities. Researchers say you can have an NDE without actually experiencing clinical death. Experts sometimes refer to this as a near-death-like experience or a spiritually transformative experience [STE].)

A full spectrum of colors in the garden grove, the flowers, and the surrounding atmosphere glistened with light and exceeded in beauty anything I had ever laid eyes on before. It seemed as if I was witnessing colors I had never seen with my naked eyes.

As a professional artist (my profession today and my aspiration back then), these celestial colors really intrigued me. If I could find a way to paint these colors I would, but I'm afraid that would be impossible. (I know, because I have tried many times, yet failed to do so.)

21

Remember

All of the plant life and the glorious, sunlit sky seemed to radiate their own light and pure intelligence. Everything had its own vibration (similar to music) that I could feel and comprehend throughout the experience. It was as if all creation was in the attitude of praising God without ceasing.

I could also hear continuous heavenly music, including a choir singing praises to their Creator, but I could not tell what direction it was coming from. I think the choral music was all around me. An overwhelming feeling of peace and joy beyond description seemed to emanate from this strangely familiar place. Everything I was witnessing was somehow connected; it was as if it was One and I was a part of that Oneness.

When I would focus on a particular object, such as a flower, I would comprehend and experience everything about it—from how it was created and by what power it was made to everything and everyone who had smelt, touched, or appreciated its beauty. I could feel the joy the flower had in the measure of its creation when it pleased all those who appreciated its beauty.

A small, organically straight, and well-worn, narrow footpath intersected the center of the grove and continued beyond and deeper into the forest. This tiny grove looked like a familiar and favored place for many to visit.

I found myself leaning face-first against a large stone near the base of a few aspen trees that were on one edge of the grove and next to the footpath. Although I was eight years old when I had this experience, in the vision I was represented as a small and innocent child of three or four years old. I perceived this representation to symbolize the life I lived before being born into mortality. It was as if I went back in time into a pre-earth spiritual dimension. Perhaps I had once stood in that very spot in times past. Maybe it was a favorite place I frequented in my premortal state to quietly meditate or prepare for my future mission on earth.

While in this dimension, my own perception of things seemed heightened far beyond my eight-year-old understanding. It was as if pure

22

Russell Ricks, *Pathway through the Aspens*, oil on panel, 6 in. × 12 in.
Painted from a trail leading up to Silver Lake in American Fork Canyon, Utah.

intelligence continuously flowed to my mind, and I comprehended many
things in an instant. Whatever I focused on, I could learn *and* experience
everything about it. But once the vision closed and I awoke, I could no
longer retain the specific knowledge I had gained; I could only remember having felt an incredible increase of knowledge.

There is, however, one thing that has stayed with me all these
years—an actual knowledge, and not just a belief, in the existence of
God, the premortal existence of man, and our continued existence after
our mortal bodies die.

Before I had this experience, my parents had taught me about God
and my spiritual premortal existence. I believed what they taught me,
but after this experience I knew, and still know, with absolute certainty
that it is true.

Though I was in a place of pure joy and happiness, my face was
buried in my hands. I was leaning against the stone in tears. I knew I
must continue on the path beyond the grove, but for some reason, I felt
a great deal of anxiety, and I hesitated. I then perceived that the mortal
world was just beyond the grove, and if I embarked on the path, I would
go beyond the point of no return, and I would be born on earth.

As I held back, I wasn't confident on how well I would do in mortality and fear overtook me. Moments later, as I lay pressed against the stone, I felt a gentle touch on my right shoulder, accompanied by a gentle and calming voice. "Russell," the personage called me by my given name, "Why are you crying?" I was taken by surprise and I remember thinking, yet not fearing, *Who is this person who knows me by my name?*

Turning back over my right shoulder, I saw a being in a long, white, flowing robe standing in the air, a few inches off the ground. His hands were exposed a little above His wrists, and His robe's hem touched the tops of His feet. A glorious (but nonblinding), white light, brighter than the sun, radiated from His being and flooded the surrounding grove. His radiance was brightest nearest His personage. His thick hair—white and shoulder-length—was neatly groomed; He wore a full, white, neatly trimmed beard. His most striking and curious feature to me was His eyes, which seemed to appear as if they were on fire and yet they were not. Remember, this was how I perceived His eyes as an eight-year-old. (Later, I will comment more on what I discovered regarding this striking feature.)

I perceived clearly that this personage was my Savior, Jesus Christ, as witnessed by His wounds, which pierced His hands, wrists, and feet (see D&C 93:1; 110:3). He looked into my eyes with great understanding, love, and compassion. He seemed to be able to look deep into my heart and soul. I felt no fear when He pierced my soul—only pure love and perfect acceptance. His voice was gentle, yet like the rushing of mighty waters, and when He spoke, He communicated telepathically. I do not recall seeing His lips move as He spoke. Perfect love—pure and unconditional—emanated from His personage. I felt complete acceptance. The power of His love encompassed everything, filling my heart with indescribable peace and joy.

His love felt similar to the witness of the Holy Spirit when it finds a place in your heart, yet this feeling far exceeded the power of the Spirit in any instance that I have ever had in my lifetime. It reminded me of the joy the prophet Lehi must have felt after partaking of the fruit of the tree of life (see 1 Nephi 8. See also 1 Nephi 11:21–23; Revelation 2:7).

We learn from 1 Nephi 11:21–23 that the meaning of the tree of life is a representation of the *love of God*. It was because of this love and joy that I hesitated to leave this happy place. Everything in my surroundings was filled with the love of God, His light, and His truth. This pre-earth life had been my happy home for perhaps eons of time. For the first time in my spirit's existence, I was about to embark on the unknown. I would have to walk by faith in God, without beholding His presence in mortality.

Sometimes, when I feel the Lord's Spirit (sometimes referred to as the Holy Ghost), it is a gentle reminder of feeling the love of the Savior when I was in His presence.

In His compassion, the Savior stooped down to lift me up and bring me to His bosom. As He did so, His robe fell open a little, revealing what looked like a wound in His side. He then gently scooped me up into His arms, carrying me off to a beautiful, distant, and radiant city above the clouds. We traveled a great distance through a pillar of light, in an instant, to the city.

Many of the buildings, the wall surrounding the city, and the streets appeared to be constructed in the purest yellow-gold! Gloriously indescribable prisms of light (again with numerous brilliant colors I had never before seen), emanated from the entire city. Even the heavenly light itself seemed to be alive and reflecting the glory of God, while singing joyful praises to Him. Here, the power of the love of God penetrated everything and overwhelmed my soul with pure joy!

I perceived this city to be near the throne of God. Perhaps it was the celestial kingdom (see 1 Corinthians 15:40–41; D&C 76:70, 96). Of all the buildings in this vast celestial city, two of them caught my attention. One appeared to be similar to the design and architecture of the Salt Lake Temple. Another adjacent structure looked like the Salt Lake Tabernacle. Except they both appeared to be constructed of pure gold material.

The Savior brought me into the Tabernacle. We went inside, discovered we were alone, and sat down on a pew near the front. Lovingly, and with His arm cradled around me, the Lord again gazed deep into my soul, inviting me to express my fears. His presence was so loving and peaceful. I felt no fear of Him.

Having great anxiety, I expressed to Him that although I understood the plan and the purpose for entering mortality, I wished I didn't have to leave. I felt that the place where I now resided was my real home and was where I truly belonged. I seemed to have had somewhat of an understanding of many of the future trials and tests I would have, to endure. Perhaps the abuse I would face in the future throughout mortality was one of the reasons I hesitated, and even feared, entering the mortal sphere. Perhaps I was also aware of the two disabilities that I would have to learn to live with.

In life, it is often very difficult to leave home for a great length of time—leaving behind loving associations with family, close friends, and the precious memories attached to those relationships. Leaving my heavenly home—my first home—was the same and more. I believe that if the veil were removed from us today, allowing us to clearly gaze into our pre-earth life, we would immediately comprehend that heaven is where we first came from and is the place where we truly belong. I believe we would have no desire to continue our mortal journey.

Although I miss my spiritual home today, I know that mortality is a necessary part of progression in God's plan for us. So, we must continue. If, after mortality, we are worthy to enter His kingdom, it will be a joyous reunion.

The Savior wiped my tears with the sleeve of His white robe. His nature is always assuring; He is loving and compassionate. He then ministered comfort to me in the form of blessings and a promise. In this experience, it was as if I was gazing beyond the veil into my past, reexperiencing an actual, personal, and precious moment with the Savior before I entered mortality.

The Savior told me that because of what I had accomplished in my first estate (pre-earth life), I was blessed. For my mission and purpose in mortality, I would be born into an LDS family, having access to all the blessings, ordinances, and promises associated with this birthright. Here the Savior told me that I was chosen and loved, and that I was a person of great worth. In this experience, while being embraced in His arms, I felt for the first time in my life that I had any real value. (There is no greater feeling in life than actually experiencing the pure love of God while in His embrace.)

At school and at church, my peers called me a "retard" or treated me like I was stupid. I was left out of most social things, always chosen last for competitive games during school recess, or ignored during recess entirely, as if I was nothing but an afterthought. Would anyone feel loved after that?

I learned from the Savior that because each one of us who comes to earth chose to keep our first estate, we are all greatly valued and blessed children of a loving God. We all came from a royal spiritual birth. The Savior reminded me of His Atonement—its purpose and its power. He promised me that I would feel the guidance of His Spirit and His companionship in my life. He also reminded me that personal prayer was a great blessing and an important tool to communicate with God. He admonished me to pray often. The Son of God taught me that through His Atonement, which He had already fulfilled, I could repent and be forgiven of the mortal mistakes I would likely make. *He then concluded with a personal promise that from time to time throughout my life, He would send messages of His love in various ways to let me know He loved me and that I had not been forgotten.*

After the Savior ministered comfort to me through the blessings and promises He personally made, He gently reminded me it was time for me to enter mortality. I took courage and faith in His promises, letting Him know I was ready to go. I trusted Him, especially because He had already fulfilled His mission while on earth and had literally atoned for the sins of all mankind. Because of His Atonement, I was reminded that through the Savior, we all had a sure way to return to God's kingdom.

We then left the Tabernacle and departed the Holy City in the same manner in which we came, returning to the beautiful, mountain-high aspen grove where my vision began. Here, we said our last farewell through a kiss and an embrace, and then I turned down the path, entering the thick of the beautiful forest where my vision suddenly came to an end.

I then awoke from my sleep, feeling the most awesome joy and having a sure knowledge that God, Himself, had held me in His holy arms and let me know He was aware of me, and that I was dearly loved by Him personally! I wanted to tell the world what I had just experienced. I wanted to tell them the amazing things I had learned and tell them all about the heavenly knowledge I had gained. I excitedly tried to rehearse and recall this knowledge, only to be disappointed, realizing it had been blocked out from my mind.

Even though I couldn't remember those things, I was left with the sure knowledge that during my visit beyond the veil, I did experience an increase of immense spiritual knowledge far greater than all earthly wisdom or scientific understanding. I believe much of what was shown to me was symbolic, in order to help me grasp certain concepts.

There was something else I awoke with as well—the indescribable feeling and power of God's love! This wonderful gift stayed with me for several months before it dissipated. No other dream had ever affected me like that. Or was it even a dream? I'm not really sure how to describe exactly what happened. I'm not sure if my spirit left my body or not, yet I kind of lean toward the belief that it did. I am certain that I was not clinically dead. If my spirit did leave my body for a time to witness the above-mentioned experience, it must have been still connected to my body somehow. All I know was that it was definitely real and from God. That's what matters to me most.

CHAPTER 6
Putting the Puzzle Together

The Bible, on occasion, indicates that no man can or ever has seen God with his naked eyes (see Exodus 33:20), yet other scriptures show that man has seen God and lived. In the Church of Jesus Christ of Latter-day Saints, we accept the Bible as God's first testament, but we believe that some scriptures in the Holy Bible were mistranslated over time through human error (see Articles of Faith 1:8). An example of this occurred when the patriarch Jacob (renamed Israel by Jehovah Himself) "[saw] God face to face, and [his] life [was] preserved" (Genesis 32:30). Is this a contradiction, or was the previous scripture a human mistranslation as the LDS Church indicates?

Today, we have thousands of documented testimonies of personal near-death accounts, where individuals have suffered death and claim to have crossed the veil into a spiritual realm. While in this world of spirits, they were often met by a divine personage. They will tell you that the experience was "more real than real" and they were filled with a love indescribable.[1] Some even share incredible, detailed accounts of what

---

1   See "Key Facts about Near-Death Experiences," *IANDS*, accessed May 2, 2017, iands.org/ndes/about-ndes/key-nde-facts21.html?showall=1; "Facts about Near Death Experience," Dr. Piero Pariestti, *The Original Afterlife Awareness Conference*, accessed May 2, 2017, afterlifeconferenc.com /articles/facts-about-near-death-experience/; Ben Brumfield, "'Afterlife'

was going on in the physical world around their lifeless body while their spirit self floated above, observing the scene below. There are often other similarities shared between NDEs: being compelled to pass through a dark tunnel or a darkened space toward a bright light; having vast knowledge of the universe continuously pouring into one's mind; experiencing a feeling of oneness with a divine personage and their surroundings; being taken to a city of light and being told that they cannot stay, but must return to mortality to accomplish a mission on earth.[2]

There are numerous others who claim to have experienced something similar to an NDE, but without being close to death. The big question that has been on my mind for decades following my own NDLE is, "Did my spirit cross the veil, even though I didn't suffer death?"

———

One article describes NDEs in this way:

Their stories [the stories related in the books *Heaven Is for Real*, *Proof of Heaven*, and *To Heaven and Back*] are similar to those told in dozens if not hundreds of books and in thousands of interviews with "NDErs," or "experiencers," as they call themselves, in the past few decades. Though details and descriptions vary across cultures, the overall tenor of the experience is remarkably similar. Western near-death experiences are the most studied. Many of these stories relate the sensation of floating up and viewing the scene around one's unconscious body; spending time in a beautiful, otherworldly realm; meeting spiritual beings (some call them angels) and a loving presence that some call God; . . . feeling a sense of connectedness to all creation as well as a sense of overwhelming, transcendent love; and finally being called, reluctantly, away from the magical realm and back into one's own body. Many NDErs report that their experience did not

feels 'eve more real than real,' researcher says," *CNN*, April 10, 2013, www .cnn.com/2013/04/09/health/belgium-near-death-experiences/.

2   See "Characteristics of a Near-Death Experience," *IANDS*, accessed May 2, 2017, iands.org/ndes/about-ndes/characteristics.html.

feel like a dream or a hallucination but was, as they often describe it, "more real than real life."[3]

—

My experience happened back in 1966, just after I turned eight years old. I knew nothing about near-death experiences until about 1975 when I read Raymond Moody's book *Life After Life*. After reading this first NDE book, I was surprised and excited to find striking similarities between Moody's book and my own experience. I discovered that I wasn't alone. In fact, I began to wonder if the experience I had was much more than a divinely inspired dream or vision. If my experience was in fact a dream, and not a full-fledged NDLE, then why did my event share an abundance of similarities to an NDE? My experience seemed just as hyperreal to me as those who had died and returned. Every time I have shared my own event with a clinical-death NDEr in person, we seem to understand each other and connect on the same level. It is always much more difficult to share something as indescribable as an NDE with someone who has never experienced an NDE. Each time I would have a conversation with an NDEr, I always ended up asking myself, "Did my spirit also separate from my body, although I still felt a connection to it?"

We've heard the phrase, "They've finally decided to pull the plug," when the decision is made to take a person off of life support. But is it necessary for the spirit self (soul or conscience) to be physically "plugged into" the body in a similar way? Or does the spirit self have the ability to temporarily separate from the body, yet still be connected in some way? I invite you to keep the plug analogy in the back of your mind for a minute and consider the following theory.

Just a handful of years ago, the dream for all electronic devices to become wirelessly connected seemed far-fetched, if not impossible. The

---

3   Gideon Lichfield, "The Science of Near-Death Experiences," *The Atlantic* (April 2015), www.theatlantic.com/magazine/archive/2015/04/the-science -of-near-death-experiences/386231/.

concept seemed beyond our current understanding. Today, this dream has become a reality, and many devices are now wireless.

There is also a device that allows users to recharge their device anywhere using Bluetooth. Knowing that it is possible to wirelessly connect to a host, is it possible that our spirit body could have a similar type of ability, if not more? Are not all things possible with God?

——

In our past, there are recorded biblical accounts of prophets, like Paul in the New Testament, who were unsure as to whether they were "in the body, or out of the body, [they could] not tell" (2 Corinthians 12:3). Like Paul, the contemporary LDS Prophet Joseph Smith Jr. also experienced this same dilemma after receiving a vision of the celestial kingdom of God (see D&C 137). I had the same dilemma when I finally returned to the awareness of my physical self.

Before Joseph Smith's vision of the celestial kingdom, he describes being personally visited by angelic beings: former Old and New Testament prophets and apostles, ancient American prophets, and also by God the Father and His resurrected Son, Jesus Christ (see D&C 137:3, 5). Each time the Prophet Joseph Smith was visited by a divine personage, his physical body would need to undergo a temporary change in order to withstand and survive the presence of a celestial being. If this is true and the physical body can temporarily transcend, how might this happen?

The scriptures give us some clues. Christ invited His three head apostles—Peter, James, and John—to climb to the top of the mountain known today as the Mount of Transfiguration. Transfigure means to "transform into something more beautiful or elevated"[4] or to change to a higher state of glory.

In the book *Encyclopedia of Mormonism,* there is a definition of transfiguration:

---

4   *Oxford Living Dictionaries,* s.v. "transfigure," accessed May 2, 2017, en.oxforddictionaries.com/definition/transfigure.

Transfiguration for mortals consists of a temporary physical and spiritual change, allowing them not only to behold the glory of God but to enter his presence. It is characterized by illumination of countenance such as Moses experienced (Moses 1:11; Ex. 34:29–35) and comes about by an infusion of God's power (*MD*, p. 725). Because God is a being of transcendent glory, it is impossible for men and women to enter his presence without their physical bodies being spiritually "quickened." The Prophet Joseph Smith explained that God "dwells in eternal fire; flesh and blood cannot go there, for all corruption is devoured by the fire. 'Our God is a consuming fire'" (*TPJS*, p. 367; cf. Heb. 12:29; Deut. 4:24). Transfiguration bestows on individuals a temporary condition compatible to that of deity and allows them to see God face-to-face.

Modern revelation says that "no man has seen God at any time in the flesh, except quickened by the Spirit of God" (D&C 67:11).[5]

It was at the top where these three apostles witnessed a miraculous manifestation of the Spirit (see Matthew 17).

———

With wireless connections, the closer we are to the Bluetooth source, the greater the reception. Perhaps the same is true with our physical bodies? The closer we are to the veil of heaven, the clearer His revelations are to our spirit within. If the spirit or soul has the ability to separate, perhaps this could explain why inspiration often comes to an individual through the medium of dreams.

I have always been in awe of how similar my experience is to an NDE, because what I experienced was so hyperreal and so much like an NDE. After all these years of pondering on this subject, I have come to the conclusion the term "NDE" is really a misnomer. It's kind of like a Xerox machine. After Xerox Corporation made the first copier, competitive companies came out with their own version of the copier, yet we still called these new machines Xerox machines. I have come to the belief

---

5   *Encyclopedia of Mormonism*, s.v. "Transfiguration," accessed June 9, 2017, eom.byu.edu/index.php/Transfiguration.

that the so-called near-death experience is one and the same whether the person dies or not, because these experiences share many common similarities. As mentioned in the preface, the scriptures refer to this experience as "being caught up" (taken up) or being "carried away by the Spirit" (under the power and influence of the Spirit).[6] NDE is a modern term created by man. When a person dies, then returns to life, the body is temporarily changed through death, and when a person is transfigured, the body is temporarily "changed" under the power of the Spirit. Since both are temporary in nature and both share a pattern of common traits, I believe both *are* the same.

I've outlined the remarkable classic similarities on the following page, comparing my experience with the standard NDE.

---

6   In the Old Testament, see 2 Corinthians 12:2, 4. In the New Testament, see Revelation 17:3; Revelation 21:10. In the Book of Mormon, see 1 Nephi 11:1, 19; 3 Nephi 28:13. In the Pearl of Great Price, see Moses 6:64 and Moses 7:27.

STANDARD NDE[7]	MY EXPERIENCE
Moving from darkness to light	Lifted up through the darkness toward a distant light
Being "somewhere else," in an otherworldly place	Being in a dimension not on earth, yet experiencing a feeling of déjà vu
Meeting with sacred figures	Being in the presence of Christ
Experiencing rapid observations	Comprehending and experiencing everything in an instant
Communicating telepathically	Communicating telepathically
Feeling the love the sacred figure has for the NDEr	Feeling the boundless power of God's love
Seeing unusual colors[8]	Seeing colors never seen before
Making a decision (sometimes unwanted) to return to the NDEr's body	Making the (initially unwanted) decision to return to mortality
Seeing cities and other objects within the initial bright light	Visiting a city of light

---

7   "Characteristics of a Near-Death Experience," *IANDS*, accessed April 27, 2017, iands.org/ndes/about-ndes/characteristics.html.

8   Jonathan Zap, *Crossing the Event Horizon: Human Metamorphosis and the Singularity Archetype* (Boulder, Colorado: Steam Press, 2012), 66.

Many researchers say that a large percentage of NDErs tend to return with some kind of supernatural phenomenon they didn't possess before. A good example is those who seem to interfere with electronic devices such as computer screens going haywire when the NDEr comes near a computer or when the NDEr's watch won't work properly when they put it on.[9]

Some claim to have psychic powers.[10] A friend of mine seems to have an enhanced gift of discernment—the ability to read the hearts and souls of individuals. He now seems to see others more as God sees them.

For the majority of individuals who return with gifts they didn't possess prior to their NDE, they say this enhanced state usually only lasts for a period of about three years. My "gift" was the ability to daily have the indescribable power and feeling of God's pure love ensuring and reminding me that He did love me and was keeping His promise!

After NDErs "return to normal" and their gift leaves them, most struggle with adjusting to returning to their life as it was before. They also struggle for a time with finding some spiritual direction that fills in, equals, or replaces the empty gap they feel inside after having an NDE.

I remember struggling with the wish that I could have stayed in the spirit realm. I thought, *Why was I sent back to face this terrible life?* How do you replace such an event in mortality after experiencing the other side of the veil?

For me, the LDS doctrine of the plan of salvation, the LDS modern-day scripture, and the related revelation from authorized LDS apostles and prophets answered, and continues to answer, most of my questions better than any other resource I have found.

Over a century before NDEs became a household term, LDS doctrine taught that we existed in a spiritual dimension before mortality—as literal spirit offspring of God—with our spiritual Heavenly Father and Creator. The LDS faith also teaches that we were born into mortality

9   "Aftereffects of Near-Death States," *IANDS*, accessed May 2, 2017, iands .org/ndes/about-ndes/common-aftereffects.html.

10   Ibid.

with a specific purpose and mission to accomplish. Regarding what will happen after we leave mortality, LDS doctrine often parallels many classical similarities between most authentic NDEs. After having my NDLE, the LDS faith satisfied my need to find a parallel spiritual direction to fill in the empty gap I felt.

Online, my experience is described by NDE researchers as a Spiritually Transformative Experience (STE).[11] I connect this to the miraculous phenomenon described in the scriptures as "being caught up by the Spirit" (see 1 Nephi 11:1). I prefer the scripture interpretation over the scientific one—it's more accurate, and it more simply describes the sensation.

———

Where did we come from? Why are we here in mortality? What happens to us after we die? Is there evidence that our individual lives have purpose? How do I find out what my own purpose is, and where do I look for these answers? These are common questions that we all ask ourselves eventually. Do the holy scriptures give us clues to help answer these pondering questions? Yes!

After having such a remarkable experience, I began to thirst for more knowledge about the above questions. I wanted to know everything I could about life beyond the veil. I picked up the Book of Mormon and read it from cover to cover, then I reread it, and reread it again and again and again.

I discovered some amazing passages of scripture within the book's pages. Hands down, my favorite section was in 3 Nephi, where the Savior, as a resurrected being, makes a personal visit to the Nephites and Lamanites who survived the great destruction in their native land. I cried when He showed compassion on them; it allowed me to relive the love and compassion the Savior gave to me. I felt one with the experience when the Savior had the children brought forward and declared the

---

11   "Russell R Experience," Russell Ricks, *OBERF.org*, accessed April 27, 2017, www.oberf.org/russell_r_ste.htm.

words, "Behold your little ones!" and angels came down from heaven encircling the little ones in fire (3 Nephi 17:23–24).

In 1 Nephi chapter 1, the ancient prophet Lehi is caught up in a vision while he pleads to the Lord in prayer for his people. As he was praying, a pillar of fire came down and "dwelt upon a rock before him" and "he saw and heard much" (1 Nephi 1:6).

After having this experience, Lehi was "overcome with the Spirit" (1 Nephi 1:7). Exhausted, he went home and lay upon his bed. Again, the heavens opened while Lehi slept and "he thought he saw God sitting upon his throne, surrounded with numberless concourses of angels in the attitude of singing and praising their God" (1 Nephi 1:8).

Reading the Book of Mormon further, I learned that two sons of the prophet Lehi, namely Nephi and Jacob, "saw my Redeemer, even as I have seen him" (2 Nephi 11:2). The scriptures teach us to liken the scriptures to ourselves; and, as I did so, I fell in love with the Book of Mormon.

In due process, my testimony of the living Christ increased. This was one of the blessings the Savior promised me that I would gain by being born into an LDS family. I have come to know, on a very personal level, the Savior's love and concern for me.

At the commencement of my full-time missionary service for the Church of Jesus Christ of Latter-day Saints, I got on my knees and pled with the Lord to know with absolute conviction if the beloved Book of Mormon was indeed the word of God, along with the Holy Bible and other revealed scripture.

I had already come to know that God was real. This left me no doubt that I would get the answer I sought. After much pleading, fasting, and wrestling in the Spirit for a period of about three days, I came to *know* that my favorite book was from God! A powerful witness of the Spirit swelled with a quiet yet powerful warmth in my heart and overcame me with inexpressible joy! A feeling I had come to trust, similar to the ineffable love I felt in the Savior's presence, flooded my soul. I know the Book of Mormon is the Lord's second witness of the testimony and life of Jesus the Christ, and I cannot deny it, "neither [dare] I do it" (Joseph Smith—History 1:25).

Because I was raised in the Church of Jesus Christ of Latter-day Saints, I grew up learning and believing that we were not just born into mortality without existing in some form before. I believe we are literally children of a loving God—God the *Father*.

I believed and knew of this reality long before I had my NDLE, and the scriptures are replete with examples of this simple truth. I didn't need the experience to convince me that we once lived in the presence of God before entering mortality. I didn't need it to convince me that God lives, and that He is an individual personage who knows me and loves me personally. I already believed this somewhere deep inside my soul. I am filled with so much gratitude that He chose to send me such great joy and comfort at a time in my life when I truly needed the type of love only He could provide.

Since that awesome, sacred night—that night I cried myself to sleep with tears of sorrow, yet awoke with a feeling of hope that flooded my heart with inexpressible joy—I no longer felt alone and unloved in this world. I continued to be abused, bullied, and teased by those around me, but I had been given a rare gift from God, and I knew that I was loved by Him personally, even if I was not loved by everyone else. This new knowledge helped me to survive those difficult years.

———

I have also recently found comfort reading in the Doctrine and Covenants, which teaches that great blessings can come to us when we bear our challenges with patience and long-suffering. In Doctrine and Covenants 58:2–4, we read,

> For verily I say unto you, blessed is he that keepeth my commandments, whether in life or in death; and he that is faithful in tribulation, the reward of the same is greater in the kingdom of heaven.

> Ye cannot behold with your natural eyes, for the present time, the design of your God concerning those things which shall come hereafter, and the glory which shall follow after much tribulation.
>
> For after much tribulation come the blessings. Wherefore the day cometh that ye shall be crowned with much glory; the hour is not yet, but is nigh at hand.

An intriguing question you might ask yourself is, "Did we each have a similar personal interview with the Savior, just before entering mortality?" I believe we did. I can't imagine my experience being one of a kind. God loves all His children and is no respecter of persons. Did He personally make covenants with each of us, and did we make a personal promise to Him that we would be obedient? This would be consistent with the way things are done in His restored Church. We have an interview with the appropriate church authority before serving a full-time mission or accepting any other major calling. I shared this idea (that we each had an interview with the Savior) with a relative, who suggested, "Not only did we have that interview, but I can picture having His hands laid upon our heads to give us a blessing, foreordaining us with special blessings and gifts, before we embarked on our mortal journey." I wholeheartedly agreed!

The Bible also gives us some clues about our spiritual state before mortality. In the book of Jeremiah, the prophet of the same name learned that he not only existed in the presence of God before being born into mortality, but that he was also foreordained to be one of the Lord's representatives.

> Then the word of the Lord came unto me, saying,
>
> Before I formed thee in the belly I knew thee; and before thou camest forth out of the womb I sanctified thee, and I ordained thee a prophet unto the nations. (Jeremiah 1:4–5)

This is what LDS apostle Orson Pratt suggested, regarding a possible one-on-one interview with Christ:

If we ever dwelt there, it is altogether likely that God made some promises to us when there. He would converse with us, and cheer us up. Being his offspring—his sons and daughters, he would not be austere and unwilling to converse with his own children, but he would teach them a great many things. And all this will be familiar to us. We read in the New Testament that God did make promises to us before this world was made. I recollect one passage in one of the epistles of Paul, either to Timothy or Titus, the Apostle says, "In hope of eternal life, which God, who cannot lie, promised before the world began." To whom did he make that promise? I contend that we had the promise of eternal life before the world began on certain conditions—if we would comply with the gospel of the Son of God, by repenting of our sins and being faithful in keeping the commandments of God.[12]

Not only is Christ intimately acquainted with us, but He has not left us alone in mortality. The Savior is aware of our needs and sends "[His] angels round about [us], to bear [us] up" (D&C 84:88).

---

12 Orson Pratt, in *Journal of Discourses*, 15:250.

Chapter 7
Miracles of Angels

I learned many years ago that the Savior never goes back on the promises He makes to us. Our Heavenly Father knew His Son could be trusted to take upon Himself the role of the Savior of mankind. He knew how much His Son loved, and still loves, us and therefore would not back out of giving His life for us. Christ spent His entire life continually striving to obey and fulfill His Father's will.

The Savior's love for us individually reaches beyond our time in mortality. During our premortal existence, I believe the Savior promised each of us that He would not fail to accomplish the Atonement in our behalf. Christ was born to die so that we might live.

Throughout my life, Christ has blessed me with His tender mercies and has kept His promises to me. I have often felt His presence near. Sometimes it's through the soft whisperings of the Spirit. Sometimes, the Savior reveals His face in more miraculous ways. Examples of this are expressed in the following stories from my past.

———

Every few Saturdays (back when Dad ran his sign business), we would load up the garbage from the shop into the back of Dad's pickup and drive to the landfill. On one particular early, slushy, snowy Saturday morning, Dad pulled me out of bed, bellowing in his false macho gruff voice, "Get out of bed now and take the garbage to the landfill or I'm going to fire you!"

Shortly after I rose from my bed and got dressed, I told Marty what Dad had asked us to do. After a quick breakfast, Marty and I went about our task.

I had only been a licensed driver for a few months. After my fifteenth birthday, I passed the written test and then qualified to get behind the wheel in driver's ed. With my summer birthday, I had never driven in snow. I have to admit, I was very nervous to get on the snow-covered road in that weather, but I tried not to show it so I wouldn't frighten my younger brother.

There was a heavy metal ladder rack on the truck, loaded with a four-inch-by-twenty-foot iron pipe. The twenty-foot pipe was not tied down and rolled freely only a few inches between two sets of vertical pipe, which were designed to keep ladders in place. I figured the pipe would be okay, and the extra weight would give me good traction on the roadway.

About a mile and a half west of Rexburg, the road bends to the left, to the right, to the left, and then right again in an S curve. I hit the due west stretch, traveling about forty-five miles per hour, then began to pump my brakes to slow down a few hundred feet before the first curve. The truck started to fishtail, but pumping the brakes kept it somewhat under control. It was then that I heard a loud, very clear, and distinctly male voice, "Russell, there's a truck up ahead and it's going to hit you!" I then saw an image in my mind of a truck pulling a long trailer loaded with hay.

I turned to my brother and asked, "Marty, did you say something to me?"

He gave me an odd look and said, "No. Why?"

"I heard a voice!"

Marty looked at me like I was crazy. The voice was distinct and very clear to my ears, as if someone sat right next to me with a deep, audible, booming voice.

On approaching the crest of the first curve, an Irish setter dashed out into the road right into my lane. At the same time, a diesel pickup, pulling an eighteen-foot trailer filled with hay, exactly as I saw it in my mind, came around the bend headed my way. My whole life flashed before my eyes in a split second. I panicked, slamming on the brakes and forgetting to press down on the clutch. Everything went into slow motion for a few seconds. Our pickup slid into the oncoming traffic, and Marty and I knew our lives would end right there!

To avoid us, the other driver did some quick thinking. Instead of maneuvering his vehicle into our original lane and potentially causing another accident from an unseen vehicle approaching, he steered into the shoulder on his side, avoiding a head-on collision with us. Unfortunately, he had to swerve to his left again to avoid hitting a power pole. When he maneuvered to the left, his hay trailer hit the driver's side of our pickup. The end result looked like a rolled-up, opened sardine can. The twenty-foot pipe on our ladder rack bounced off and landed on the other driver's hay trailer, splitting it down the middle lengthwise and scattering hay bales all over the highway.

In spite of being quite shaken up with all that had happened, I was grateful to God that I was alive, and even more grateful that my brother was unharmed. As soon as I could, I went to the nearest house to make a phone call home. I was in tears and bawling when Dad picked up the line. I just knew I was going to "get the frozen boot" for what I had done, but when I explained with fear the details of the accident that had happened, Dad spoke softly, "Oh really? Are you okay?" I bawled even harder, surprised that my dad didn't give me the tongue-lashing I expected!

Dad later got his sweet revenge on me by forcing me to chauffeur him in the pickup everywhere he needed to go. This, he said, "Was to teach me a lesson never to wreck another vehicle he owned." I can't say I learned that lesson very well.

—

As I think about it, I am reminded of a few other times when God sent His ministering angels to my aid when I desperately needed His divine intervention. One of these experiences happened when I was still a small boy.

My father, my younger brother, and I were on our way to Jackson Hole, Wyoming, from the Idaho side; we were driving over the Teton Pass. I don't recall the purpose of our trip, but since Dad was an artist and a sign painter at the time, it likely had something to do with that. Marty and I were invited to tag along. I was only ten or eleven years old at the time, and Marty was around the age of eight or nine.

At the top of the pass, one of the tires went flat. Dad removed the spare tire that was fastened to the undercarriage of the big Chevy family van and got out his tire iron and jack. He then proceeded to jack the car up. After it got up to a certain point, the jack started to slip out of place. The van began to sway and teeter a little. I wasn't watching, but I think Dad tried to knock it into place, and that is when it fell on him, pinning his body underneath.

From where I was standing, I couldn't see how my father was pinned when he screamed for help, but my brother and I acted quickly. I said a little prayer, and the two of us wimpy little boys lifted up the back bumper with all our strength. Somehow, we were able to raise the van up enough that Dad was able to get himself free. I have no doubt that God's angels were also helping us that day. We all knew that what had happened was a miracle! We were so grateful to God that day.

—

I mentioned earlier that I served an evangelical mission for my church. I shared our message with the people in central California. On one occasion, when I was still a new missionary and "wet behind the ears" (I was what my fellow missionaries called a "greenie"), I had another inspiring experience.

My missionary companion, Elder John, had been out just over nine months. Elder John was my senior companion and was in charge. We were both to serve as missionaries for two years, at which point we would return home and resume our regular lives, including college, dating, and sports.

Due to recent weather conditions, we had been unable to go out and knock on doors to look for people to teach and had been holed up in our apartment for about two weeks. It had been raining big buckets of rainwater steadily in Oroville, California, day and night; so we were unable to go door-to-door to find those who wanted to hear our message.

I was bored and getting very frustrated. I felt useless, and I was anxious to do the Lord's work. About all we did was read and study our scriptures, write in our journals, and listen to the radio. Not that those were bad things—I just felt we should be doing more.

While listening to the radio one particular rainy morning, we heard the annoying long, high-pitched tone that comes before the National Weather Service report, warning us of potentially dangerous flash flooding. Oroville was just a few miles below an earth-filled dam. The radio announcer reported, "There is a flash flood warning now in effect for Oroville and the surrounding area. The reservoir above the Oroville Dam is full to overflowing and in danger of collapse! This is the worst rainy season we've had in decades. Be prepared for flash flooding and prepare to evacuate the area!"

Naturally, I was very concerned by that announcement. When I was seventeen, the Teton Dam, an earth-filled dam in southeastern Idaho, collapsed and sent a fifty-foot-high wall of water down the canyon. By the time it hit my hometown in Rexburg, Idaho, the wall of water was three to four feet deep. I watched many homes get pushed off their foundations by the incredible force of the water. Many homes, businesses, and farms were completely destroyed in the wake of the devastation.

I expressed my concern to Elder John, suggesting that we ask the Lord to stop the storm. John declined. He said, "I believe the Lord works by natural means. It is not our place to call on the Lord's power to stop the storm."

I was not satisfied, and I was not about to go through another "Teton Dam disaster," so I kept insisting we get on our knees and petition God. John then said, "Okay, Ricks, you say the prayer!"

I told him I felt it was worth a try and I would say the prayer, so I did. We got on our knees and asked the Lord to stop this dangerous storm so we could get back to work. As soon as we said "Amen," all we could hear was the rainwater trickling down the rain gutters on the sides of our apartment!

We stepped outside and looked up. The clouds had parted and the sky had cleared within what seemed like a few seconds. It was almost like the parting of the Red Sea in the classic movie, *The Ten Commandments*.

On the radio, the announcer was so astonished he became almost speechless, wondering exactly what had happened. Only moments before, he had sent out a severe warning to his listeners. We knew it was God who answered our prayer! We knew His ministering angels were surely watching over us. I also knew that the Savior was keeping His promise to me. I was greatly humbled.

The storm was stopped, not by my power, but by God's power. I knew the Lord would be by my side as I served in His great missionary work. This single experience greatly fortified my faith in God.

———

Many years later, on another very rainy day, I experienced a moment when I knew God was watching out for me and my family. At the time, I was married to my first wife. My dad had turned his sign business over to me, and it was now my full responsibility.

On one particular rainy weekend, I had a large bill that was past due and needed to be paid. Because of the weather, I was worried that I wouldn't get an outdoor football stadium sign painted, meaning I wouldn't get the money in time to pay the bill. If I could just finish the football stadium sign I had started a few weeks previous, it would be an easy $800 and would more than take care of the debt.

I had asked the Lord in prayer for help to get the debt paid and put my faith in Him. I knew from the experience that I had on my mission that he could answer my plea and calm the weather on my behalf once again.

The morning started out raining, but by early afternoon, the weather had started to clear. I quickly loaded all my supplies up in the sign truck and hurried as fast as I could to the job, about forty-five miles away. As I drove, I prayed and prayed hard.

Every few moments, it looked like it would start to rain again. Not only did I have to paint the sign, but the sign also needed time to dry after I painted it. By the time I got to the job site, put up my ladders, and started to do the job, I could see a storm heading my way.

Oh no! I thought, and I began to plead with God in earnest for help. I asked the Lord to please let it not rain on me so I could finish the job. I knew I would be there a couple of hours.

As the storm closed in, a miracle occurred and my prayer was answered. The whole time I painted the sign, it rained all around me, but something very unusual happened. In a radius of about eight hundred feet, with me in the center, it did not rain! I was able to finish the job and collect the payment for it a few days later.

———

On another occasion, a few years after I first married, I asked my father-in-law if he would organize a trail riding trip to the Bechler area in the southwest corner of Yellowstone National Park so I could take pictures of the numerous waterfalls for future paintings.

The Bechler area circles an approximate thirty-mile radius. Within the Bechler area, it is estimated that there are over two hundred waterfalls along the Falls River. I asked if my father and my brother Jeff could also come along. It would take at least one week or more to take pictures of all the falls on the trail. Our focus would be on the two most famous waterfalls: the Colonnade and the Iris Falls.

A few weeks later, the trip was organized and we set off on a Friday afternoon for the Bechler area. Our group consisted of my father, my father-in-law, Jeff, and a friend of my father-in-law. We made camp that evening at the head of the trail. That night I had a dream that I was riding my father-in-law's horse, Mary Jo, on the Bechler trail to Colonnade Falls. (In reality, I had never seen the falls before, not even in a picture, but when we got there the next day, they were clearly the falls I saw in my dream.)

In the dream, I tied Mary Jo to a tree near the edge of a cliff and held onto the reins with my right hand, while handling my 35mm camera with my left hand. It would have been a "perfect picture." I felt it was worth the risk, so I tried my best to proceed carefully. I was so close that the mist and spray from the falls wet the grass, the rope I held, my camera, and my face.

The next thing I knew, I saw myself slip off the edge and plunge to my death at the foot of the falls. The four others who had joined me on the trail soon noticed I was missing, found Mary Jo still tied to the tree, and surmised that I had fallen to my death or drowned. They searched for my body for a few hours, but their search turned up nothing.

My dream ended there, and I woke up in a cold sweat. Early the next morning, I told my dream to the others, who all agreed it was a clear warning from the Lord. Still determined to get some good pictures for future paintings, I insisted on going and promised to be careful.

That afternoon, when the trail opened up to the falls, I saw the exact spot from my dream where I had been warned not to go. Because of my warning, all of us stayed away from that area.

Once again, I was so grateful for the Lord's warning, sparing my life. A few months later, I turned out a successful painting of the waterfall.

———

Let me share one more miraculous story from my experience as a missionary.

The last area I served in, prior to my return home, was one of the highlights of my whole missionary experience. I was assigned to the Clayton Valley, California, area the final six months of my two-year evangelical commitment. Once again, I witnessed firsthand the protective power of ministering angels.

In this area, my missionary companion, Elder Thompson, was traveling ahead of me on his bicycle at a high speed. I was having great difficulty keeping up with him, and was quickly falling far behind.

When he passed through an intersection up ahead, the light was green. By the time I reached the same intersection, the light had turned red. On my approach to the changing light, I witnessed a miracle.

As Elder Thompson passed through the intersection, he had the right-of-way. A teenaged driver, on the opposite side of the intersection and on Thompson's right was not paying attention to the traffic. His car rolled forward as he focused on a young woman crossing the street. It was at that moment that I knew Thompson and his bike would be hit, sending him hurtling through the air.

Instead, his bike's back wheel miraculously lifted up off the ground about four to six inches and moved to the left about one foot, narrowly escaping and avoiding the car altogether. Through all this, Elder Thompson somehow maintained complete control of his bike, coming to a stop a few dozen feet past the intersection.

By the time I caught up with him, I shook my head and asked, "How could you have possibly done that 'trick' on your bike at such a high speed without getting hit and still manage to maintain control?" Thompson then said, "That wasn't me!" Both of us realized that we witnessed the ministering of angels in our behalf. God truly watches over His servants. He always remembers and watches out for His faithful missionaries.

I have had many other experiences where I have received more than coincidental warnings and protection from a divine source, but they are too numerous to mention. What I have shared with you in this chapter are some of the major ones I can recall.

It is my knowledge and assurance that the Lord truly does love us, knows us by name, and watches out for each of us. We can all feel the ministering of angels throughout our lives. I know that God loves each of us and is very aware of our existence. He truly knows us personally and is interested and concerned for our welfare. We are never alone, and sometimes God reveals Himself to us in quiet ways.

—

One day, while reading the scriptures, early in my missionary service, I was reading in section 110 of the Doctrine and Covenants. This section is a revelation that Joseph Smith Jr. (a prophet of the restored gospel of Jesus Christ) received during the dedication of the Kirtland Temple to the Lord. Doctrine and Covenants 110:1–4 reads,

> The veil was taken from our minds, and the eyes of our understanding were opened.
>
> We saw the Lord standing upon the breastwork of the pulpit, before us; and under his feet was a paved work of pure gold, in color like amber.
>
> *His eyes were as a flame of fire; the hair of his head was white like the pure snow; his countenance shone above the brightness of the sun; and his voice was as the sound of the rushing of great waters, even the voice of Jehovah saying:*
>
> I am the first and the last; I am he who liveth, I am he who was slain; I am your advocate with the Father. (Italics added)

I was overjoyed when I read this! This passage, particularly verse three, was a perfect description of the personage I intimately witnessed during that miraculous experience eleven years previous. I knew this was not a coincidence. I also understood by the Spirit that this was the Lord's way of keeping the promise He made to me during my time with Him in the premortal realm.

In the above verses and with a few simple words, Joseph Smith clearly described the divine personage I saw! That personage was Jesus Christ! I knew that God was watching out for me, even as He had promised.

This scripture fortified my belief that the experience I had beyond the veil was not just an imaginary dream. It was much more than that. It was clearly a message from God, showing that Christ was keeping His promise. It was a divine gift from my Heavenly Father, and it had deep spiritual meaning for me—a meaning that has taken me many years to understand, and I am still learning new things from it. The experience also filled my heart with a desire to draw closer to Him, feel His love, and bring me to repentance when necessary.

Discovering these verses in Doctrine and Covenants 110, further fortified my desire to understand the meaning of the vision. I now believe it was because I desperately needed to know and feel pure love and comfort after suffering so much abuse from my peers and others. I was shown that I was a person of great worth who was personally known and loved by God. In the process, I came to know the reality and personal nature of an infinitely loving God.

I had also experienced aspects of His Atonement. Christ suffered agony beyond description in the Garden of Gethsemane and on the cross so that He could understand and feel my pain and suffering and your pain and suffering. Because of His loving sacrifice, Christ is the only being who could completely succor my sorrows and heal my inner wounds.

In the process of discovering the meaning of my experience, I also learned to trust in His Spirit and recognize His handprint in my life. I have come to know that all things truly testify of Christ and, once you are aware of this, you can find His handprint in your life and everyday surroundings. Some things are obvious, like the miracle of an innocent newborn baby straight from heaven. Other things are less obvious, yet you can discover His divine signature if you diligently and prayerfully search for it.

While reading the Doctrine and Covenants further, I discovered Joseph Smith's vision of the celestial kingdom in section 137. Once again, I found another remarkable passage of scripture similar to my own experience:

The heavens were opened upon us, and I beheld the celestial kingdom of God, and the glory thereof, *whether in the body or out I cannot tell.* (Italics added)

Just as I have concluded with my own experience.

I saw the transcendent beauty of the gate through which the heirs of that kingdom will enter, which was like unto circling flames of fire;

Also the blazing throne of God, whereon was seated the Father and the Son.

I saw the beautiful streets of that kingdom, which had the appearance of being paved with gold.

I saw Father Adam and Abraham; and my father and my mother; my brother Alvin, that has long since slept. (D&C 137:1–5; italics added)

Here it was again, another witness of the Lord's handprint. His tender mercies in my own life were pointing directly to my own experience. I was overcome with wonder, joy, and awe.

CHAPTER 8
A Miracle in the Lord's House

A few years later, after having returned from my mission for the Church, I married my first wife. After I had been married for perhaps a year or two, I had a remarkable experience in the Idaho Falls Idaho Temple. An LDS temple is a very sacred place. In temples, we are schooled in the things of God, and we perform sacred ordinances for ourselves and for the dead.

Because of the sacredness of the temple, there are many things we cannot and do not discuss outside its walls. Inside we make sacred covenants with God, the details of which we do not discuss because they are so personal and hallowed.

What I am about to share is not part of the temple ceremony, but it is very personal and sacred to me. I only share it here for the purpose of this account, because it clearly points to my experience beyond the veil. Here it was again, another of the Lord's tender, loving mercies in my life.

While I was meditating and enjoying the abundant feeling of the Spirit that flooded the celestial room, I was admiring the mural painted on the four walls. It suddenly dawned on me that the artist had clearly depicted some of the symbolic things that were shown in my NDLE.

After I entered into the celestial room and found a place to relax, I sat facing two entryways. I noticed that painted on the wall between the two openings, there was a cluster of aspen trees with a large stone at its base. I was overcome with joy and desired to know the personal meaning behind the mural. I asked myself, "Why didn't I notice this before? Surely the experience I had in my youth was from God!"

To my surprise, a similar scene was painted on the wall across the room. This wall was between two entryways to sealing rooms where celestial marriages, lasting for time and all eternity, are performed. This further fortified the truth of my new discovery!

In my vision as an eight-year-old boy, I perceived the stone and cluster of aspen trees to perhaps symbolize a marked passage similar to a portal separating the world of spirits and mortality. I also considered it to be an altar; a place where I had tearfully offered up a broken heart and a contrite spirit, fearing I would have to leave that sacred place where I felt safety and pure love.

As I began studying the mural more intently, I also noticed another symbol that had been shown to me in my own experience. In one corner near the ceiling, the artist had painted a celestial city in the clouds. All the buildings were painted to appear as if they were made of gold, and two of the buildings looked very familiar. One building was painted to depict a replica of the Salt Lake Temple and the other resembled the historic pioneer tabernacle on Temple Square in Salt Lake City, Utah.

One other representation in the temple mural was very personal, although it was not part of my NDLE. The artist, Lee Greene Richards, had added several figures, representing spirit children of our Heavenly Father who had earned the right to enter God's kingdom. Two of the figures very closely resembled my Grandma and Grandpa Hunter (my mother's parents), who had passed away a few years previous. One sitting figure reminded me of my beautiful mother when she was younger.

To me, this was another divine handprint that what I had experienced in my NDLE and witnessed in the temple mural was not a coincidence. Nothing could have been tailored more personal than this! It almost seemed as if God had the artist paint those symbols for me!

Some skeptics might call it a coincidence. I will tell you that it was rather unlikely, if not impossible for this to be a coincidence, especially after witnessing the examples I shared in the previous chapters. Being a skeptic by nature with many things, I wondered this myself at first, but after a temple is dedicated, tours to the temple interiors are closed to the general public. After that, only members are allowed to enter. Even then, in order to qualify, members must prove their worthiness first through an interview with their LDS bishop and receive a temple recommend.

I had never been on a temple tour before my adulthood. This mural was painted more than a decade before I was born, but I was not aware of it until I noticed the significance of the mural approximately thirteen years after my baptism. There were some books in my family library about temples. Going through all of them, even turning the pages carefully one at a time, I found that none of our books had pictures of the celestial room in the Idaho Falls Idaho Temple.

One of the most illustrated books on temples in our family library had several photos of temple interiors. It even had pictures of some of the wall murals in the Los Angeles California Temple, but none of them depicted similar scenes like the Idaho Falls celestial room interior. Each celestial room temple mural is hand-painted and unique.

After my temple session was over, I found the current presiding president of the temple, Elder Devere Harris, sitting in his office. I asked if he had a moment to answer a question. He let me in, inviting me to sit down. I shared my NDLE with him and the relationship of my vision to the murals in the celestial room. After I finished relating the experience, I said, "I believe the artist was inspired!" I then asked him if he knew what it all meant.

Elder Harris responded, "First, I want to let you know that, yes, I know the artist was inspired, and second, you should know that you're not the first one who has had such an experience. There have been others who have had a similar experience."

He also said he couldn't answer what it all meant, but offered that someday I would understand when the time was right. I left the temple filled with unspeakable joy and gratitude, knowing that I was not alone! There were others out there somewhere, others who had had a similar experience and were perhaps searching for the same answers. I left his office, even firmer in my testimony that we truly existed before we were born and we will continue to live after we die. I also left with hope that I would find some of those people who had had a similar experience to mine.

I find it interesting that there are others who had a very similar Idaho Falls Idaho Temple story with him. Whatever it was that happened to me, the same may have happened to others.

I recently spoke to a gentleman (Mr. Little) at a meeting for the International Association for Near Death Studies (IANDS) in Salt Lake City, Utah. Mr. Little told me that many years ago, someone else shared a similar Idaho Falls Idaho Temple experience with him, confirming Elder Devere Harris's words.

As you may recall, I have previously mentioned that I believed much of what was shown me during my NDLE was symbolic to help me grasp certain concepts. At first, most of the symbolism was hidden from my understanding, but over time, my understanding began to unfold a little at a time.

Something also drew me to the aspen trees, the large stone, and the pathway. During the event, I felt that these three objects had deep symbolic meaning for me personally. The Savior himself taught in parables and analogous parallelisms to protect the gospel mysteries from those with proud and hardened hearts, while making them plain and simple to the humble follower who had eyes to see, ears to hear, and hearts that could be penetrated (see D&C 1:2). To the proud, the Lord's ways are foolishness, but to the humble and teachable, the Lord's use of symbolism gives His gospel a deeper and richer meaning.

For example, although we preach about and worship Christ, the chapels of LDS meetinghouses are typically void of painted images or statues representing the Savior or other saintly figures. The walls and architecture of LDS chapels are simple in design; but, hidden in the architecture, you can often find layers of subtle symbolic meaning and representations of the Atonement, the sacrament, the three degrees of glory, the gathering of Israel, the Godhead, and more.

In my own meetinghouse, two stained glass windows were designed with symbolic representations of the tree of life, which represents the love of God. I love our chapel and the profound symbols I find there.

For many years, I have tried to understand what the Lord wanted to teach me when He granted me a vision beyond the veil. I have since concluded that it was because I needed to feel a genuine love from the true source of love, so I would know that I counted as an individual and that my existence mattered. I've also come to understand that I was born with disabilities and struggled socially. Then I was granted that vision to teach me to be more compassionate, loving, forgiving, and nonjudgmental and teach me to try harder to view others like God would see them.

I have always felt that the artist, Lee Greene Richards, was inspired when he painted the mural in the Idaho Falls Idaho Temple. The temple president assured me that he knew that Richards was given the heavenly inspiration to paint it, and that there have been others who have also experienced something similar relating to the mural.

For years I have pondered this idea, and wondered if Richards and others had a similar experience. How similar was it? For many years, I have searched, pondered, and prayed to know the answer. I have diligently searched the Internet. I even spent a day in the LDS Church History Library. While in the library, I discovered that, yes, the artist did create and present a rendered concept for the Idaho Falls Idaho Temple celestial room, with many of the same images that showed up in my dream. But, I was not allowed to view or handle the sketches due to the sensitive and sacred nature of the archived document. It also had not and would not be photographically digitized for public use.

On the evening of June 17, 2015, I prayerfully approached the Lord again during a sleepless night and took to the Internet. This time, I came across an interesting statement found in a book titled *Hidden Treasures of Ancient American Cultures.*

In reference to the artist Lee Greene Richards, the author stated,

> One who knew his talents well [an unidentified person] claimed that "Brother Richards' talent is really a spiritual gift, in that he often paints what he has seen in dreams or visions." That was apparently the case with his most intriguing mural, then located "on the southerly part of the west wall" of the Celestial Room in the Idaho Falls Temple. It inspired more comments from Latter-day Saints gathering in and passing through this room than any other temple mural. (When the temple was closed down for a year of extensive remodeling, from September 1972 till October 1973, it was removed and a less inspiring mural substituted in its place.)[1]

Were some of those individuals who commented on this mural among the others that the temple president said had a similar experience? Are some of these individuals still alive today? If so, I hope to find them.

During part of the extensive remodeling in the early 1970s, the celestial room ceiling was lowered about eighteen inches, covering up part of the Holy City originally painted by the artist. When I discovered that the image of this city was the same as in my dream, this ceiling had again been raised and the mural restored to its original concept.

> The original mural "showed heavenly buildings" suggesting a holy city . . . coming down out of heaven." One of the later temple presidents explained to some of the temple workers, while they stood in front of this marvelous mural, that "it was the City of Enoch and the righteous people with him." When someone once asked Lee Richards how he happened to come by way of that particular scene, the artist explained that it had come to him in a vision one time and remained present long enough for him to capture enough of the details of it. Later, when the First Presidency commissioned him to do some murals for the Celestial Room, the inspiration came to him to paint the scene from the vision of Enoch's City.[2]

---

1   John Heinerman, *Hidden Treasures of Ancient American Cultures* (Springville, Utah: Bonneville Books, 2001), 143.

2   Ibid.

Along with coming to know the reality and inexpressible feeling of God's boundless love, I also learned that God always keeps His promises. For that reason, it is important that I remain humble and worthy, accept His will in all things, and obey all of God's commandments (not to pick and choose, thinking some don't apply to me) if I am to receive the promised blessings He has for me on conditions of repentance.

Because of God's amazing grace and His miraculous gift of a selfless atoning sacrifice, I *can* become what God wants me to become! Undeniably, my NDLE also has played a role in helping to shape and fortify my belief in the reality of God and the pure truths found in the restored gospel of Jesus Christ.

Other examples of God's timing, miracles, and handprint in my life are outlined in the remaining chapters. Through these examples, I hope to paint a clear picture showing that God never goes back on the promises He makes with us.

CHAPTER 9

Tender Mercies of the Lord

One of the priesthood offices in the Church of Jesus Christ of Latter-day Saints is that of a patriarch: a Melchizedek Priesthood holder who is called and set apart by a modern-day apostle of the Lord, and is given sacred keys and spiritual gifts from God. This office and calling is like those of the patriarchs of the Old Testament—Abraham, Isaac, and Jacob. A patriarch has the gifts of prophecy, seership, and revelation. They can give worthy members of the Church a patriarchal blessing. A patriarchal blessing is like a blueprint, outlining important events, promises, and blessings in your life if you keep God's commandments.

I received my patriarchal blessing when I was fifteen years old. Patriarchal blessings are very personal and sacred to a Latter-day Saint. Like many holy things that occur in the Lord's holy temple, we are asked not to casually share the details of our patriarchal blessings with everyone.

Let me just mention that my patriarchal blessing makes a couple of statements that refer to the miraculous vision I had as a young boy. The patriarch who gave me the blessing knew nothing of my vision beforehand. It's also interesting to note that I have received many other priesthood blessings from various priesthood holders over the years when I was sick or discouraged. They also knew nothing of my experience; yet, in many of these blessings, they expressed similar things referring to my dream. How else would they have known this except through the Spirit of the Lord as they were prompted on what to say?

I wonder sometimes if my experience was a parting of the veil or if it was a literal gaze into the past of an actual event—a very real personal moment with the Savior. For me, sacred moments like these are part of God's tender mercies. They are His way of fulfilling the promise He made to me in the premortal existence; the promise that He would take the time to let me know He loved me personally and that I am important to Him.

It is so wonderful to know and feel that God really cares about us, watches out for us, and is always there when we need Him. My patriarchal blessing further indicates that I would feel the Savior's companionship throughout my life. This, undeniably, has been true. Since my mission service and frequently throughout my life, I have most often felt the Savior's unselfish, loving presence through the Holy Spirit, whose divine task is to bear witness of Christ.

Have you ever been sitting quietly and then softly and seemingly out of nowhere, the Spirit of the Lord gently floods your soul, beginning with a soothing, peaceful, warm sensation in your chest? This is one way the Holy Spirit comes into our hearts to testify of Christ's truths or to bring comfort to our souls. One memorable time when I felt the Lord's presence nearby, and perhaps the closest since my NDLE many years ago, was on a difficult night of tragedy that led to another miracle.

CHAPTER 10
Starting Over

There are always two sides to a failed marriage relationship. They say that somewhere midway between the two perspectives is closer to the truth. I have no desire to offend or hurt anyone, especially my children and grandchildren. I honestly hold no resentment or anger toward my ex-wife for the past.

At the same time, and for the purpose of this chapter, I want to try to express some of the pain I was going through, how I hurt inside at the time, according to how I perceived things twenty years ago, *but not necessarily how I perceive things now.* I apologize in advance for exposing such raw feelings on my take in my divorce, now over twenty years ago.

My former wife is remarried and seems to be much more settled and happy than before, which makes me very glad for her. The following is an attempt to express some of the turmoil I felt back then, followed by how I felt the Lord's loving hand during this period.

Today, twenty years later, I have been able to let it go. I have since forgiven those whom I felt hurt by. They are all wonderful individuals.

Beginning with the experience I had as a small boy, followed by many tender mercies pointing back to the experience, I have learned that the Lord is always there for me. The Savior has always kept His promises, just as He promised me as a child. I no longer have any reason to feel alone. I know I can rely on Him and trust His will, despite my trials. He has always been there for me in one way or another.

One of those periods in my life came when I was very much in need of His loving embrace and healing balm. He came to me as I was on my knees for several hours one night in fervent prayer.

My first wife had filed for divorce. This was one of the most difficult and heart-wrenching trials I had ever faced at that time. Fifteen years of marriage with my first wife would be officially, and sadly, coming to an end the following day. In the LDS church, we believe that marriage and the family unit are sacred and eternal. Sacred ordinances inside a Mormon temple seal a husband and wife and all their children to each other for time and all eternity. This means that we can all be together as a family unit in the next life, not just for our time here in mortality. Families can be forever. Most religious faiths have lost and don't teach this pure principle of truth, although many of their patrons believe it in their hearts.

After a long period of struggling to salvage our relationship, and then finally realizing she no longer loved me and that we wouldn't be able to change the circumstances, I finally gave in to her demands for a divorce. This of course devastated me, mostly because I would no longer be with my children 24/7 like I had been.

My small sign shop and art studio were next to our home, so my children had been able to come and talk to me whenever they chose. This was the way I grew up, with my dad having his shop behind the house. That had also come to an end.

I was in such a bottomless, depressing depth of sorrow. I couldn't be comforted. I felt like the world itself was collapsing all around me. (Three months after the divorce, I was also grieving from the death of my father. That was even harder to bear, to carry both burdens.)

The night before my divorce was finalized, I was on my knees for nearly six long hours, pleading with the Lord to try to make my wife have a change of heart. As I fervently prayed, I heard God's familiar voice in my mind. God let me know that He loved this daughter of His.

He told me to step aside, move on with my life, and He would handle it from here. After hearing this, in my selfish heart, I felt that the divorce was so unfair. I felt that I had been wronged. I was not happy to hear this, and I let the Lord know that I felt hurt and angry, feeling that what happened to me was so unjust.

The last few years prior to our divorce, due to our communication challenges, I had struggled with a constant state of severe depression, and I just couldn't pull myself out of it. Not fully understanding the things I was doing wrong back then, I would get so frustrated trying to find a way to make my wife happy.

During our marriage, I struggled with feelings of complete rejection and insecurity, both in public and in private. I was also depressed because I felt like I was shunned by some of her family as a result of my choice of profession in the visual arts. This made me feel unworthy of their approval. They seemed like nice enough people, yet under the surface, I felt a lack of approval, real or imagined.

It wasn't until I moved to Utah almost two years after the divorce that I was able to begin to remove the shackles of the emotional and physical pain I suffered from my earlier years as well as the depression from my failed marriage. I hold no anger or bad feelings for this good family now. They really are good people. Who is to say their take on life wasn't valid? They were just watching out for their daughter.

After I pled with all my heart to the Lord for a miracle to fix my marriage, a miracle did occur, but it wasn't the way I would have pictured the outcome—I thought my life was over.

The Lord had another path in mind for me, just not the one I would have expected. I only ever wanted to be a good person, a good husband, and a good father. I just couldn't understand why she felt different about whether or not our marriage should continue.

As I look back now, it *really did* come down to one of those clichéd "irreconcilable differences" situations. No one was really at fault or very happy in the relationship, but I wanted to fix it through marriage counseling. I still believed it was possible. She just couldn't go on. She couldn't bring herself to go with me.

She and her family were raised so differently from the way I grew up, yet I felt love for all of them. Although I considered her my childhood sweetheart, other than our children and our religious beliefs, we really had nothing else in common. I felt that was at least a good place to start and a good place to start over, especially since we had already invested so much. She expressed that those two things were not enough, and she couldn't go on any further.

I even gave up aggressively marketing my artwork through galleries for a while. I went to college and focused on the sign business full-time, to try to appease and compromise with her and her academic-minded family. That sacrifice didn't seem to change things.

Looking back, I realize now that she needed more of a friend than I had the ability at that time to be. I wasn't able to be the friend she longed for, though I honestly thought I had really tried. Even though I knew I struggled daily with communication skills, I did love her. Somehow, I guess I just couldn't communicate what I felt for her in my heart.

Now I realize that due to two challenges I struggle with daily (one of which I was unaware I had at the time), I was unable to communicate effectively. Those challenges were at the center of my lack of social skills. It really was no one's fault. Perhaps God did have a purpose for us joining together in the first place—to parent our seven amazing children. Otherwise, they would not have been born to us or would have been sent to other families. I consider their birth an amazing miracle and a blessing!

To make a long story short, the marriage was over the next day. I was at peace in the way that I tried to put the pieces back together; I felt right with my efforts before the Lord. I did everything in my power to convince her to reconsider, but she had her agency and still said no.

An amazing miracle occurred the night before the marriage ended, but not without an extremely difficult and emotional inner struggle. As I poured out my soul, the Lord let me know that there really was no real justified reason it should come to an end, but she couldn't go on; she was entitled to her agency and had made up her mind to end the marriage. I was advised to move on with my life. There was no turning back.

For the space of what seemed like four or more hours, I felt the chastisement of the Lord. Although the Lord said (as I heard His voice in my mind) that there was no real reason the marriage should end, there were many mistakes I had made that hurt our relationship—little things. Many of those things, I suppose, were sins of omission, little things I should have done, but didn't do.

What I learned from this experience was though my mistakes were "little" in my own mind, in her mind, that was certainly not the case. I learned that what I considered to be little things were really big things.

Communication was a big one. I should have somehow communicated better. In my frustration, I did try, but I had no clue where or how to start. Even after fifteen years of marriage, I was still so naive. Much of it was likely because of a disability I didn't even know I had. Socially, I was so far behind everyone else. I didn't even realize I was not connecting the dots in the way that everyone else communicated. I really had no clue.

I didn't even begin to have a clue until about the age of fifty, twenty years later, when I discovered I was born neurologically different than the average joe. That difference was clearly at the center of my challenge to communicate with my former wife and with others. When I found out about my major disability after an MRI scan, I immediately began to seek treatment for it.

Although originally it was a big shock, this new awareness has been a relief for me in one respect: I was able to get very good treatment by some very capable professionals. My current wife and family all say I am doing much better than before. But I'm also human and still slip up once in awhile.

The most difficult thing I have ever faced in my life was feeling the Lord's wrath that night before the divorce was final. Before then,

I thought going through the divorce was the most difficult. Boy, was I wrong!

When the reprimand (which seemed boundless or endless) finally came to an end, I thought my life was over, replaced with hopelessness. I found out I was wrong about that too!

The sun would be appearing over the horizon soon. My marriage would officially end in a few hours, and I was no longer allowed to be around my children 24/7—only on scheduled days. The thought of being apart from my kids was the worst! I could adjust to bachelorhood; I just couldn't bear not having my kids around me like before.

Since I had to move out, my studio and sign-shop workspace moved as well. In the process of making that change, a strong impression came to me to turn to the Bible. As I did so, the pages fell open to a passage where I read, "For whom the Lord loveth he chasteneth" (see Hebrews 12:6). This was followed by a distinct and gentle voice in my mind (that familiar and comforting voice), "Your life isn't over. There's a plan B in place. I have something waiting for you in Utah!" Then in a flash, I saw a face—a woman with locks of white hair and blue eyes!

There wasn't just something waiting for me in Utah, there was a beautiful someone. Was the Lord truly preparing the way for me to meet my future soul mate in the near future?

Elder D. Todd Christofferson of the Quorum of the Twelve Apostles taught, "Divine chastening has at least three purposes: (1) to persuade us to repent, (2) to refine and sanctify us, and (3) at times to redirect our course in life to what God knows is a better path."[1]

Despite the reprimand I had just passed through, a feeling of peace and inexpressible joy swelled up inside my soul! My life wasn't over after all! It was just beginning! The Savior, who had twenty-nine years earlier put His gentle, loving arms around me and told me I was loved by Him and promised me that He would keep in touch, had once again let me

1 D. Todd Christofferson, "'As Many as I Love, I Rebuke and Chasten,'" *Ensign*, May 2011.

know that He loved me! I was given a second chance at doing things better and I wanted to do it right.

I spent the next few days getting my life in order: paying off old debts and burying the hatchet with the offended, all in order to get myself square with God the very best I could.

A few days after receiving the Lord's chastisement, I felt I was ready and worthy enough to move forward, requesting a clean slate in spite of the past. I got on my knees, pleading with God and fully believing that He would answer my prayer. I had done everything I could think of to repair that which was in my power to get right with God.

Even though my efforts didn't immediately fix everything, I knew I had done what the Lord required. I had done my very best. With some people, no matter what I did to make it right, I could never measure up in their eyes. I knew that their opinion of me may never change. I did my very best. I would have to move on, and the rest would be up to God.

As I poured out my soul to God, I felt completely ready to request His forgiveness. I prayed that He would accept my efforts and asked Him to remove the heavy burdens pressing on my heart and weighing down on my shoulders. In a way that I cannot explain, my burdens were completely removed, followed by an impression that I had been fully forgiven. I truly felt the amazing power of God's grace through His Atonement. He had already willingly suffered the burden of my own sins for me personally. My sorrow was replaced by the most exquisite joy—a feeling similar to what I felt across the veil. For a brief moment, I even thought that I again felt Him place His loving hand on my shoulder, just as He did that miraculous night many years before!

Before I was born, the Savior promised He would let me know I was personally loved by Him and would feel His companionship. I desperately needed to feel His love. I felt His presence before me right there in the room. I relished in the warmth, peace, and joy that I felt, afraid to open my eyes for the longest time for fear the feeling would go away.

For the next several weeks, I again carried the most incredible sensation of joy. Many people noticed a change in me and commented how happy I seemed in spite of the divorce. Indeed, I was happy. The incredible feeling of God's love, similar to what I had experienced on the other side of the veil, had returned. I was carrying it inside again and relished it. Christ's Atonement had personally taken effect in my life. I learned that His saving grace is real though an inexplicable power! As a result, I was overcome with unspeakable joy!

I looked forward to the day when my soul mate and I would finally meet, but I was in no hurry to move. I couldn't abide putting that much distance between myself and my children. I was also still running a small sign business with loyal customers. I couldn't drop the business. Some of the work was boring, but every once in awhile I would do something fun like hand-letter, hand-pinstripe, or airbrush a semitruck or customized auto. Once in a while, I'd even get a painting commission.

What I really wanted to do was paint full-time again, selling to important art collectors through art galleries. But my emotions were in so much turmoil at the time that I couldn't even lift a brush to a canvas. It has taken me years to get into the right groove again. Now that I am, my work is ready. I am pursuing my art career again with enthusiasm.

While still in Idaho, I would often find a blank wall or two to paint a mural on. Painting murals was one of my favorite creative pursuits in the sign business, next to creating fine art for art collectors. But the murals didn't make me any money back then. I usually went in the hole during my Idaho mural period. (Since that time, I have been blessed to paint more lucrative mural projects for important clients like Cabela's, Alcoa, Novatek, and others.)

After the divorce, I was trying to make the best of it and move on with my life. A few weeks later, an individual said some painfully offensive things about me. Instead of ignoring their hurtful words, I took offense, got very angry, and eventually found myself outside my faith. It's unfortunate what stubborn pride can do.

I let my anger influence my behavior, instead of being more level-headed and forgiving toward the individual. The anger swelled within me. Not long after, I stopped attending church and I stopped praying, turning my back on my religious upbringing, because I let the offensive words of an individual hurt me. From my angry and judgmental viewpoint, I began to look at others of my faith as hypocrites, and I used this as an excuse to fuel my anger and stay away from church.

I'm a realist. Even though I was judgmental toward a small number of Latter-day Saints, I *knew* this was a small and isolated circumstance. It was not a reflection on Church membership as a whole. It was my arrogant and judgmental point of view toward a small handful of individuals. You can't judge the entire organization by the actions of a few of its members.

Yes, there are bad apples in every crowd, but that gives me no right to judge them. God would want me to love them instead. What made it so hard was that I had once considered some of these people to be friends and some were former family members.

In spite of the fact that I had felt the Savior's pure love and embrace as a small boy and knew the reality of His existence, and in spite of the fact that I had experienced the power of Christ's atoning sacrifice for me personally as an adult, I chose to step away from church ties for a while to try to sort my life out. That was a huge mistake.

Eventually, I fell into a bad relationship with a woman who was far removed from my previous religious standards. I even rationalized in my mind and tried to convince myself that I was really happy. Yet, deep inside my heart, I knew my falsely perceived happiness could never compare with the joy I knew as a small boy. Nothing in this life could ever compare with or replace the joy I felt in God's presence. That's why so many NDErs struggle adjusting to reality when they return to life; this life cannot compare to what they experienced.

It also became harder and harder to visit my children on a regular basis. Whenever I did, issues left over from the divorce would sneak in and get in the way, ruining the visit, and my children would get hurt. Ugly rumors and lies would spread their vicious poison. Nothing seemed to be working out in my life at that time. Life seemed so off-balance and unfair.

For about a year and a half, I allowed anger to fuel my heart. I drifted further and further away from my spiritual roots. Although I stopped going to church during this period, I never doubted my earlier experience. I still had a spark of a testimony of the gospel, and I knew what had happened to me as a child was authentic. God really did answer a little boy's desperate prayer in his time of need.

I no longer felt worthy of that experience. I knew God was real, yet I no longer felt worthy of His love. I struggled to put my life back together without calling on God for help. It was a very dark period in my life.

Feeling the weight from all my sorrows, I drifted farther and farther away, until I was no longer living according to the standards I had been taught. I felt so lost. I thought I was beyond the hope of the Savior's loving grace. I began to miss the blessings I had previously had. I began to miss being worthy to feel the Lord's Spirit. I wished I could be that innocent, little eight-year-old boy again in the arms of the Savior's embrace.

After a while, I finally mustered up the courage to go to my LDS bishop and start turning my life around. I eventually broke off my relationship with the woman I had been seeing and began to work with my bishop who helped me put my life back on track.

Several months later, my oldest son asked me to ordain him to the office of a priest in the LDS church. Because of my sincere progress, my bishop granted me a special recommend to ordain my son. I prepared myself through fasting and prayer for three weeks prior to giving him this blessing. My biggest concern was that I wanted to be able to invite the Spirit. I wanted the Spirit to help me speak the words of the blessing and not allow bad feelings to distract from this opportunity. My prayer was answered. The Spirit was there, and I was truly assisted by the Lord, despite the possibility of bad feelings. The Lord gave my son a powerful blessing!

I also knew that the Lord had forgiven me for my past offenses. The individual who had previously offended me even commented on the powerful feeling of the Spirit that was in the room during the blessing.

I was grateful that she identified and acknowledged this. It helped me begin the process of forgiving her.

Each of us have our own set of weaknesses, shortcomings, and faults. Although we may sometimes feel justified, it is not our place to judge. I also know that the Lord has asked us to be forgiving of all men—no exceptions—even if we may feel completely justified at times.

In Doctrine and Covenants 64:8–11 we read,

> My disciples, in days of old, sought occasion against one another and forgave not one another in their hearts; and for this evil they were afflicted and sorely chastened.
>
> Wherefore, I say unto you, that ye ought to forgive one another; for he that forgiveth not his brother his trespasses standeth condemned before the Lord; for there remaineth in him the greater sin.
>
> *I, the Lord, will forgive whom I will forgive, but of you it is required to forgive all men.*
>
> And ye ought to say in your hearts—let God judge between me and thee, and reward thee according to thy deeds. (Italics added)

On those occasions when we might even be justified in our own minds, the Lord still requires us to forgive, so that our souls might be "sanctified and cleansed from all sin"[2] and thus be completely worthy of God's love and mercy. In the Lord's wisdom and mercy, the Lord has balanced the scales when unjust trials are unfairly heaped upon us. Remember,

> For verily I say unto you, blessed is he that keepeth my commandments, whether in life or in death; and he that is faithful in tribulation, the reward of the same is greater in the kingdom of heaven.
>
> Ye cannot behold with your natural eyes, for the present time, the design of your God concerning those things which shall come hereafter, and the glory which shall follow after much tribulation.

---

2   Leonard J. Arrington, "Oliver Cowdery's Kirtland, Ohio, 'Sketch Book'," *BYU Studies Quarterly* 12, iss. 4, (1972), scholarsarchive.byu.edu/cgi/viewcontent.cgi?article=1533&context=byusq.

For after much tribulation come the blessings. Wherefore the day cometh that ye shall be crowned with much glory; the hour is not yet, but is nigh at hand. (D&C 58:2–4)

God is always a God of mercy, fairness, and justice. We must forgive "all men" (see D&C 64:10), including those who have been the cause of so much pain. Any injustices that need righting, the Lord has promised will be made right in His own timetable. There will be a far greater, more exquisite reward than the suffering heaped upon us while in mortality. Exaltation will eventually be crowned upon us if we endure our trials with faith and patience.

I believe that the purpose of trials and tribulation in our lives is to cause us to change for the better. We can either choose to get angry and become rebellious, or we can allow affliction to commit us to improve ourselves and overcome bad habits. We can either hold grudges and wallow in the past, or we can turn to Christ and seek His forgiveness, allowing us to then forgive ourselves and start anew.

CHAPTER 11

Letting Go and Moving On

The last four years of my dad's life were the best times I had with him. Serving him helped me see my dad more through God's eyes and further forgive him from past hurt. I was not very close to my dad growing up because of his gruffness toward me. That all changed when he got really sick, resulting from his own poor management of his congestive heart disease. About four years before he passed away, Dad began growing even weaker, eventually getting to the point where he was too weak to continue to do many things on his own.

Dad was once a stocky man, weighing over 250 pounds. At the climax of his illness, he became frail, weighing only about 98 pounds. I would drive the ten plus miles to his home nearly every day, and sometimes twice a day, to help him lift or move something in his art studio.

Rather than resting, he insisted on continuing to practice his craft of painting. He had vowed to die with a paintbrush in his hand, and he pretty much did. During those times of his vulnerability and dependence on my service toward him, Dad shared many personal things with me. My service toward my dad's needs became a labor of love. The two of us grew closer during this period. It was then that he apologized for being so gruff and hard on me. His apology was accompanied with tears, letting me know he was sincere.

I had already resolved it in my own mind as an adult, before he verbally apologized. I'm grateful he was able to find the words for his own peace of mind.

When he passed away, it had only been about three months since my divorce, which added to my burdens. After he passed away, I missed not having him around to talk to. Since Dad's death, I know I have sometimes felt him by my side while I've created my art. His funeral was crowded. There was only standing room available at the back of the chapel. Some individuals came up to my siblings and me afterward and shared many stories, acts of quiet selfless service our father rendered them, with the desire to remain anonymous to the public. These individuals had kept their promise to Dad all these years while he was alive.

During my wrestle with anger, bitterness, and all the seemingly unanswered questions regarding my divorce, I learned some profound lessons. When I finally came to the realization that I didn't need to heft the weight of my heavy burdens upon myself, I instead chose to turn it over to God and put my trust in His personal promises to me.

Not all of the questions were answered back then, and some are still unanswered now. When I finally let go of and accepted the past, stopped judging those that I had been critical of, and instead chose to learn from my mistakes and trust God's timing, the blessings of God's promises began to unfold! For way too long I had carried an unnecessary burden. I finally allowed myself to move on, trusting in God that my questions would someday be resolved and that it was okay. A new chapter in my life was about to begin. Hope had returned.

CHAPTER 12
Promises Kept

God's blessings of comfort and peace offer a respite from the heavy burdens we all carry. These blessings are available to all who seek Christ's loving and healing power. After having received that wonderful manifestation of love and healing from my Savior over fifty years ago, I desperately desired to believe that I was not alone in this experience. Now I know that there are others, surprisingly many others.

NDE researchers estimate that as of 1997, in the United States alone, at least fifteen million Americans have had an NDLE in their life.[1] This shows that God exists and reveals His hand in the lives of millions of His children. He has chosen to bear His witness to millions today in a special way that shows that He lives, loves us deeply, and knows us personally. In addition, He also grants each of us gifts, witnesses, blessings, and experiences of His divine love and power, intricately tailored to meet and comfort our own individual needs.

———

I now have found many understanding friends who share with me in this amazing miracle. I discovered most of my NDLE friends

---

1   Thomas Cattoi and Christopher M. Moreman, eds., *Death, Dying, and Mysticism: The Ecstasy of the End* (New York: Palgrave Macmillan, 2015), 135.

more recently through the monthly meetings at the IANDS chapter in Salt Lake City, Utah. After I learned about IANDS back in 2012, I only wish I had discovered this gold mine of amazing people many years earlier.

Now, I can share my own story and hopefully help others find their own answers. Perhaps this was part of the reason why I felt a powerful urging to write this book. Yes, there will be those who will respond negatively to my experience, but I care most about those whom I hope my experiences will benefit.

Although this story is about me, I'm not sharing it for personal attention or to gain notoriety as some have already criticized. I know what it is like to feel so abandoned and alone, to be a social outcast, beat up by bullies frequently from school.

My purpose is to reach out to those who feel life is hopeless and unbearable, to show them that God has not, nor ever will, abandon us. I want to show them that life is not hopeless, and when we fully turn our hearts to God for help, He can show us a new and better path to follow.

In the process of writing, I learned a lot about myself. Putting my experiences, ideas, and feelings on paper caused me to ponder, look inward, and dig deep. As I took a deeper look back into my past, hindsight showed me God's loving and guiding hand in my life.

I am now grateful for the lessons I've learned from life's experiences. The following is one of the big lessons my past has taught me. If we let ourselves get hurt by something or someone, if we have unanswered questions that seem to continue to go unanswered, all we have to do is let go of our pride and acknowledge our vulnerability, realizing that we cannot carry this burden alone without God's help. We must then place our burdens upon God's altar and humbly allow ourselves to be molded as clay in His hands and in His way. Allowing God to do this, while prayerfully listening to the voice of the Spirit and searching the scriptures, can unfold miraculous spiritual blessings tailored very personally to meet our specific needs. I learned that many questions cannot be answered completely through the reasoning of our own power. We must rely on God. I have learned to trust in God's Spirit and in His timing.

One of the unanswered questions I carried for the longest time was, "Why do I have to struggle so much with basic communication, and what is it that I am missing?" I chose to trust God's timing and waited patiently for the answer. The answer to that question didn't come right away, but it did come eventually. It came after I moved to Utah.

———

I believe God sent us to mortality for a divine purpose. Each of us has a mission to fulfill. Sometimes, the only way to gain the growth and knowledge we need in this life is by going through the experience. In other words, sometimes the *only* way to know something is to truly experience it, feel it, and then allow God to guide and shape us.

It's difficult to give a logical explanation of something intangible such as faith. It is much easier for an individual to understand a concept like faith if they go through the process of exercising their faith. To understand something really well, sometimes we need to have experiences that teach us the good and the bad of a situation.

Instead of saying, "Why did that have to happen to me?" or being too quick to judge, perhaps a more effective approach would be to prayerfully reflect back and ask ourselves, "What did I learn from it?" or "What can I learn from it?" We can then embrace the lessons from the past, forgive ourselves, and invite the Savior to release our burdens.

One of my favorite chapters in the Book of Mormon is 2 Nephi 2. For me, this chapter is personal and profound. It sums up our life's purpose in very plain and simple doctrinal concepts. I would invite you to ponder on its words.

We learn in chapter 2 about the necessity for opposition in all things in life. Burdens, trials, disappointments, pains, and sufferings are a necessary part of life. Part of the reason we are here is to gain experience, to learn from our experiences, and then, in the process of the lessons learned, ultimately choose God. When we end up choosing God, we can experience true joy from the process.

The Prophet Lehi teaches us that, "Men are, that they might have joy" (2 Nephi 2:25). The only way to experience true joy is to also have experienced its opposite. Trials are a part of life. Our life's purpose is to overcome and rise above our trials by ultimately choosing to follow God. To choose God is to love and serve others, love ourselves, and also love our enemies. We must not forget that if we truly love and follow Him, we will obey His will by also obeying all of His commandments. The ultimate test in proving our love to God is to faithfully continue to trust and obey His will even when it seems like God has abandoned us. Examples of this kind of trust are found in the scriptures through the lives of men and women like Jesus Christ, Abraham, Job, Queen Esther, and others.

—

Shortly after returning to activity in the LDS church, I decided the time had finally come for a change of scenery. I hoped to further heal from the divorce and fully forgive the individuals who had offended me. I had just turned thirty-nine when I finally followed the Spirit and planted my feet in Utah. Being so many miles apart from my loved ones was so hard, but I determined to be directed by the Spirit. I chose to trust God.

My first Sunday in Springville, Utah, I attended an old chapel on Main Street. I entered a classroom early, a few minutes prior to the beginning of a Gospel Doctrine Sunday School class. The lesson was about the dedication of the Kirtland Temple, including the marvelous manifestations of the Spirit when the veil parted, angels were seen, a heavenly choir was heard, and some saw the Savior appear and others heard His voice. The scriptures relating to the lesson were found in Doctrine and Covenants section 110—the same section I had read as a missionary. This was the section that included the description of the Savior's eyes, hair, and voice—the personage I had experienced!

Before the lesson, the instructor had handed me a slip of paper with a quote on it by Elder Warren S. Snow. I was to read the quote out loud later during the lesson. As I read the quote to myself, I choked up, and was shocked by the incredible words! Being so overcome by the words and the topic of the lesson, I was afraid I wouldn't be able to read it aloud to the class members.

Elder Warren S. Snow said, "I remember when receiving my endowments in the Temple at Kirtland, I heard the voice of God as plain as I hear my own, and this testimony I have borne for thirty-one years."[2]

Miraculously, it had been *almost exactly thirty-one years to the day* since my experience beyond the veil when I was embraced by the Savior and heard His voice!

The Lord's timing is always perfect! As He had promised, the Savior once again let me know that He was watching out for me. I knew this was another message of love from Him! This message from God gave me more courage as I adjusted to my new home in Utah County. I truly needed to know from Him that I was doing the right thing and would survive the move.

I found employment working for a sign shop in Springville. My foreman was an alcoholic, and he was very temperamental. He acted jealous of my talent. The job lasted only six weeks before they let me go.

I found another job in Salt Lake City with Schmidt Signs. That job also didn't last long. I was terminated after six weeks. (The commute from Springville was horrible anyway.)

Struggling with employment, I finally signed up for temporary employment through a Utah Valley temp agency. I was able to do a variety of temp jobs for a while, but I wasn't making enough money to afford an apartment. Most of those temporary jobs were either finished in a few days or weeks, or they would "let me go" early.

---

2   Warren S. Snow in J. C. Graham and A. Ross, "Minutes of a General Conference Held in Birmingham, Sunday, January 3rd, 1864," *The Latter-day Saints' Millennial Star* 26, no. 4, (January 23, 1864).

r struggling for several months to find employment, my gener-
l compassionate older sister Becky invited me to live with her
until I got back on my feet. I appreciated my sister's generosity,
gh I felt discouraged and ashamed. Here I was, a grown man and
father of seven children, and I couldn't even hold down a decent job.
ontinued to trust in the Lord's promises, but it was hard.

During this period, I would commute from Sanpete County to Utah County working temporary employment jobs. Most of what I made was swallowed up in the cost of commuting. I felt like I was spiraling backward financially, and, in fact, I was. Things seemed to only get worse, especially after I hit a deer and my minivan was totaled on a slick, wintery road during my commute.

I managed to find a little sign work in Sanpete County for a few weeks during the summer of 1998, then in the fall, my brother hired me to work for his picture frame business in Springville. Becky and my mom located a basement apartment for me in Spanish Fork so I could ride the bus to work.

The apartment was nice! There were no cockroaches and it had three bedrooms. One bedroom became my art studio, another was for when my children came to visit, and the last was where I was supposed to sleep. Instead, in my loneliness, I would often fall asleep on the living room couch with the TV on.

During my single period in Idaho and when I first moved to Utah, I would often attend single adult activities organized by an auxiliary program sponsored by my church. Sometimes, it was nice to meet new people, but the majority of them carried a lot of emotional baggage and scars from previous relationships. I had certainly failed with my first marriage as well as the abusive relationship I had during my inactive period outside of the LDS church. Nothing seemed to be working out with this group, so I stopped hanging out with this group for several months.

When I would pray at the end of the day, I often told the Lord I was tired of trying to find a future companion on my own and I would put it into His hands. If there was indeed another someone meant for me, I wanted God to put it together.

I tried to occupy my free hours after work with painting. Normally, creating art was a spiritual experience for me and was a pleasant escape from the stresses of life, but because I was so lonely for someone special, sometimes it became hard for me to focus on my art.

Finally, after a long period of avoidance, I gave into the temptation to go and broke my vow to stay away from those scary single-adult events. I ended up attending an LDS single adult dance in Utah County one Friday evening.

During the dance, I met someone who I seemed to have a lot in common with. We danced a lot during the night as we got acquainted with each other. The next weekend, I attended the singles' dance activity hoping to find her there again. She didn't show up. I tried again the following weekend. She didn't show, and a week later, it was the same. Just like Cinderella, she was gone without a trace. I had no way to contact her—not even a glass slipper. After the third or fourth failed attempt, I was about to give up looking for her, finally asking other women to the dance floor.

One of the women I danced with was a woman by the name of Sherrie. Sherrie was bubbly, active, and fun to be around, but I could tell she wasn't my type. After all, I was no longer looking for a wife. I had given that to the Lord. I was just there to try to enjoy myself and spend time with other people. Sherrie became a good friend.

Sherrie said she knew someone she thought I would like to meet. The next night, she drove to my apartment to pick me up and take me to another dance. Since my transportation was gone (from that minivan deer incident), she would always call to invite me to an event, then swing by to pick me up. Each time she did that, I would always sit in the passenger seat up front. On this particular night, before we got in her car, she offered me the backseat. I did as she asked, but thought it was a bit unusual. It was dark, so I couldn't really see inside. When I climbed in the backseat, there was a beautiful woman with white hair and blue eyes sitting in the front seat. Sherrie introduced her as Karen Samuelson. I thought, *What is Sherrie up to? Is she trying to play matchmaker?*

As Karen and I got acquainted, I found out that she had seven children like I did. She also had professional artists in her family. One of them was her very talented aunt, Emma Randolph, who had regularly attended art workshops at my father's nationally recognized art school. Karen is also very creative in her own right. We shared many other similarities.

At the time we met, she was taking weekly pottery classes from our friend Andy Watson, a gifted and established potter. Karen would often show up to my basement apartment in her clay-smeared coveralls to watch me paint. I would join her every Thursday evening to watch her and Andy throw.

Many months went by, and we "hung out" with each other several times a week, then the night came when I proposed. On a starry night just over seventeen years ago, Karen and I were spending time together outside, talking, and looking up at the sky. As friends, we were very comfortable with each other and enjoyed doing the same things together. We had now been good friends for about eight months. I was in no hurry to get remarried and neither was she.

As we "hung out," I suddenly realized how comfortable it felt to be with her and how happy I would be if could spend the rest of my life making her happy. So, I asked her, "What do you think?"

Surprised, Karen looked at me and responded, "What do you mean, what do I think?"

Then I popped the question, "About us? Feels right, doesn't it?"

With the look of shock she responded, "Are you asking me to marry you?"

"Yeah," I said, "When I moved to this state, I told the Lord that I was not going to actively look for someone to remarry. There were too many divorced women with so much baggage, and I was tired of socializing with them. I told God that if He had someone for me, I wanted Him to bring us together in His timing and in His own way. I wanted a friend. I also prayed He would let me know without a doubt that she was the right one." I then paused and said, "It seems that moment I prayed for has now arrived, so I ask you again, what do you think? Does it feel right to you too?"

Still in a bit of a shock, she finally said, "I need some time to think about it!"

After that, I walked her home. We hung around for a few moments longer, embraced, kissed, and said goodnight.

One of the pieces of sign equipment I brought to Utah with me was an old Gerber 4B vinyl cutter, designed to cut out lettering of various sizes with an adhesive backing. On the way back home from Karen's the night of the proposal, I had a tape measure with me and I measured the sidewalk. With that measurement, I made a set of letters to install on Karen's sidewalk. I also made an even smaller set, just big enough to fit in her car's rear windshield. Each set read, "Karen, will you marry me," but the smaller set was in reverse, so she could read it in her rearview mirror.

About three in the morning, I returned to Karen's neighborhood with the vinyl lettering I had prepared that night. Each letter was of various sizes and was ready to apply to flat surfaces. I made several sets. The biggest letters were about three feet tall and read, "Karen, will you marry me?" I installed one set of these big letters in the middle of the street and one set in her driveway. I also installed the smaller set of letters on her car.

The next morning, Karen woke up to discover what I had left in her neighborhood and on her car. For the next week, everywhere Karen went in her car, my proposal went with her. Two days after I had proposed, Karen said yes!

A few weeks later, we turned our paperwork in to our church leaders to request a temple marriage. It got back to us that all the authorized leaders from our separate bishops, stake presidents, and the chain of Church General Authorities up to and including the First Presidency of the Church, all said, "We feel really good about this marriage!" This was very reassuring for us to hear.

We were married in the Provo Utah Temple on November 26, 1999. When we were first married, our blended family lived in Karen's home for about a year and a half. If I was to continue practicing my craft of visual art, I needed more space than the tiny bedroom where I worked. We also needed more room when my children came for an extended visit.

I had just finished painting a large wall mural for a client, which was a fairly lucrative temporary job. It seemed that life was getting better so we determined it was time to find another place to live and a better place to raise our big family. After weeks of searching, we found a home in rural Salem, about five miles south of Spanish Fork.

We moved into our new home in July of 2002. The house was a "fixer-upper," but it was livable. (That is, once we finally chased out the raccoons and sealed off the hole they made in the roof.) The original parcel of land where the home sat was on a three-acre plot. The real estate on this property included the house and five outbuildings. By the time we purchased the property, a couple acres had been parceled off, which resized our land to just over a half acre.

The large carport became my new studio. I loved my new studio. For the first time in years, I had enough space to hold an art class of up to ten students. I also was able to create several large wall murals on canvas for clients like the Cabela's store in East Hartford, Connecticut. That was a fun job, even though I had to burn candles at both ends to finish it.

Another one of my mural clients donated a very nice skylight for my studio. A few other clients commissioned me to paint some murals for their place of business. These projects were gargantuan in size. One of the murals was so big, I dubbed it the Godzilla mural, measuring twenty-two feet high by two hundred feet long.

Our home also included a large room where my wife taught piano. My seven children mostly lived with their mother in Salem, Idaho. When they came to stay with us for extended visits, they lived with us in

Salem, Utah, which was a fun coincidence. We loved our home and felt it had awesome potential!

We were looking forward to fixing the house up and turning it into our dream home, but then, five years later, the economy took a turn for the worst. Sadly, we ended up losing the home to the bank in 2008. Even though this was a difficult period of time in our lives, we have very fond memories of all the good times we had in this home and with the people of the Salem community. We made many good friends during the six years we were there.

The disappointment, discouragement, and insecurity I felt from the loss of our home was only one of many burdens I was carrying at the time. We had children struggling with drug addictions living at home. Gratefully, both children are now happy, thriving adults and have successfully made a complete recovery. We are so proud of them!

On top of the loss of our cherished home and these addictions, I discovered something about me personally, which left me in shock. I was very discouraged and severely depressed for several years afterward. "How much more can I possibly bear?" I would ask myself over and over.

Throughout my life, I have struggled with the challenges that come with having two disabilities. Despite my disabilities, that single tender moment I had with the Lord in that sacred forest grove has given me great comfort. In my youth, even though I had many hard times, at least I knew the Lord was with me and loved me. Let me repeat, I *knew* the Lord loved me and was with me. It was no longer just a mere belief. My elementary through junior high school years were frightening, discouraging, and miserable because I felt socially shunned by everyone. During those painful years, it never even occurred to me that there was the possibility of having something physically or neurologically wrong. I began to become aware of at least one of my disabilities around my mid-twenties.

For years, I had suspected that I had some type of hearing impairment. When I suggested this possibility to my first wife, she would discount my hearing loss, claiming I had "selective hearing" and just chose not to listen to her when she had something to say. Of course, this hurt when she said that, but to be fair, she was not the only one that said it.

In my early thirties, I decided on my own to take a hearing test. It turned out that I was right. I learned my lesson—trust your gut feelings. According to the hearing specialist, my left ear had some pretty severe nerve damage, which was most likely inherited at birth. We reached this conclusion since my mother was almost completely deaf in her left ear, as was one of her uncles.

Over the years, the severity of my hearing loss has increased. I now have serious nerve damage and loud noise damage in both ears. For example, I have a hard time hearing many high-pitched rings on a cell phone or some of the old-fashioned dial phones. I either don't hear them at all or I only hear them if you put the device right up to my ear. When my own cell phone rings in a public place, it always turns heads because I have the volume turned up to the highest level. People will usually point out to me that my phone is ringing.

I love to hear my wife Karen play songs on the piano. She plays so beautifully with expression. I am grateful that I can still enjoy many of the sounds of beautiful music, in spite of my hearing loss. I've noticed with pianos though, my ears don't pick up the sound of about the last dozen keys. I have always wondered what they sound like. My hearing aids do help a little, but only a little.

After learning of my hearing impairment, I surmised that my hearing disability was a big contributor to my poor social and communication skills. Many years later, I learned that I had reasoned correctly, but it was only a small part of the whole problem. The bigger shock hit me in my fiftieth year.

CHAPTER 13
Less Is More

Regardless of how I may conduct myself from day to day, I have come to know without a doubt that God is always aware of my needs and my desire to have Him near. If I want to feel His presence close by, I need to be doing the kinds of things that will draw His Spirit close. If ever we feel that God has abandoned us, this is not so. We are the ones who have pulled away. The invitation to let Him into our hearts again is always open and welcomed, so it is entirely up to us and the way we each choose to use our agency. If you are always found to be choosing good, God will let His presence be known.

If we ever feel like we have lost our connection, we have a good opportunity for self-evaluation. As we take the time to evaluate our standing with God, Satan and his hosts will often try to put thoughts in our heads, telling us that we are not worthy of God's love or even His forgiveness. Don't ever listen to such lies. Christ's Atonement is far-reaching and endlessly extended to all. He has not forgotten you, and He never will.

His Atonement also encompasses the lonely and downtrodden heart. After my first marriage ended, I initially thought my life had come to a screeching halt, but I was very wrong. God extended His loving hand and led me to a much better life in Utah.

—

After we lost our home in Salem, we moved to a much smaller apartment in the town of Payson. Although I was grateful that we again had a roof over our heads, I was still battling deep depression. Depression stemmed from losing our previous home, struggling with unemployment, and feeling very frustrated and discouraged over family members struggling with addiction. I also had insecurities that stemmed from the shock of a neurological disorder, and I felt pretty unmanly and of little worth.

Because work was scarce (even temporary jobs were hard to find from 2008 to 2010), it seemed I had no other option left but to apply for disability. All of this contributed to many sleepless nights. When I drove a vehicle during the day, I would sometimes fall asleep at the wheel. Since I would fall asleep, this eventually led to three car accidents that were my fault, making me responsible to pay some hefty fines in municipal court. It was hard to meet my court obligations, because money in our personal economic circumstances was very scarce at the time.

After my last car accident, I felt like I had finally hit the bottom of my bottomless pit. I was at the last strand emotionally, hanging desperately onto a tiny thread of hope that something would soon change for the better. I earnestly pled with the Lord for help, never doubting that He would hear my pleadings. I humbly begged to have some relief from all my afflictions. The relief I sought began to occur in the late fall of 2010, when I got word from one of my mural clients that he would be ready for me to paint another mural by the first of the year in January 2011.

A little more than three years before, in 2007, when the economy drastically turned downward, things seemed to be going pretty good. I was surfing the clouds on a high. I had just landed a lucrative mural contract with Cabela's. The year before that, a Provo client commissioned me to paint a large indoor mural. The Cabela's contract required me to paint five large wildlife animal habitat murals as backdrops for a new

Cabela's store in the heart of Connecticut. It was a reasonably profitable job. Four murals were painted on oversized rolls of primed cotton artist's canvas and glued to the walls of the store. To paint the African display, it would be painted right on the display wall on site. In early August 2007, Cabela's flew me to East Hartford, Connecticut, to install the four canvas murals and apply the paint for the African scene directly on the wall.

Completing the five displays from late May through early August was going to be a big challenge, so I hired out some good help to get them done. Two young relatives, with a reputation as reliable, hard workers, needed to earn some money for full-time missionary service, so I offered the temporary apprentice job to them. To keep their names confidential, we'll call them Brad and Jerry. Brad was about sixteen, and Jerry was thirteen or fourteen.

The year previous, I learned about a neurological disability that Jerry was born with, called agenesis of the corpus callosum (ACC). At the age of seven, Jerry had been having some difficulty at school. Jerry also struggled socially. Somehow, inexplicable to him, Jerry became the target of continual bullying and teasing at school. The conflicts sometimes occurred several times a week.

Jerry's mother decided to take him to a doctor, who ordered a brain scan. This test revealed that Jerry had agenesis of the corpus callosum. ACC is a "congenital (lifelong) brain abnormality that occurs when the corpus callosum does not develop as it should during the early prenatal period."[1]

In Jerry's case, he was born with complete agenesis of the corpus callosum (or cACC). This meant that the corpus callosum area of his

1   "What Is Agenesis of the Corpus Callosum (ACC)?," College of Education and Human Development, *University of Maine,* accessed May 1, 2017, umaine.edu/edhd/research/acc/what-is-agenesis-of-the-corpus-callosum-acc/. See also "Corpus Callosum Disorders," *National Organization for Disorders of the Corpus Callosum,* accessed May 1, 2017, nodcc.org/corpus-callosum-disorders/#cc.

brain appeared to be completely nonexistent. The corpus callosum portion of the brain links the pathways from the left and right hemispheres
together. This pathway allows for the brain to assimilate and process
information fairly quickly from one cerebral hemisphere to the other.[2]

In Jerry's case, the complete lack of a corpus callosum had caused
severe social delay and some learning delay. Reading an individual's body
language correctly is also difficult for those with ACC (in that they have
to put more hours and more effort into their studies than their peers).

As Jerry told me about his struggles socially at school, I began to
realize that his story was my story. He was able to cry on my shoulder
because I understood perfectly what he had been going through. I shared
my story with him, and we cried together. Now, looking back at his
life many years later, Jerry is doing extremely well. His mother is in the
medical profession. She and his family members have coached him about
proper social etiquette and have helped him learn the necessary academic
concepts needed for him to catch up with his peer group.

Jerry is very smart and is now successfully working his way through
college to earn his registered nursing degree. He is also doing amazingly
well socially.

Jerry helped me on the Cabela's mural for three weeks before returning home. After he left, Karen and I considered the possibility that I
might have a similar disability.

In order to find out if I had ACC, it would require a costly MRI
scan of my brain. Once we finished painting and installing the five large
indoor murals for the East Hartford, Connecticut, store, Cabela's was
very happy with my work and offered me the possibility of painting
murals for three or four more stores in 2008.

Besides the Cabela's work scheduled for 2008, a developer for a new
strip mall in Orem, Utah, and another private client had also commissioned me to paint murals for them.

My hopes for a record-earning year were dashed by late December
of 2007, when I received a disappointing email from Cabela's, informing

2   Ibid.

me that with the uncertainty of the current economic trend, the outdoor outfitter company had decided to temporarily halt all future plans to build new stores. The developer and private client ended up canceling the jobs I was going to do for them as well. It was almost like my work scheduled for 2008 disappeared in one night.

Looking back, I don't know how we managed to survive from the beginning of 2008 to the end of 2010. Work was scarce, yet somehow we survived.

Since I had two disabilities, applying for Social Security disability seemed to be my only option. At the time, we didn't have medical insurance, so it took nearly a full year to secure the funding to schedule an MRI. Once scheduled, the day came in early September of 2008 when I went to the radiology lab in the Utah Valley Regional Medical Center for my appointment. I was a little scared about how I might react to the outcome, but I was determined to face the music. I felt like I needed to know if my childhood struggles, as well as my current adulthood communication issues, were linked somehow to ACC.

Before they had me lie down in the MRI machine, I asked for a copy of the x-rays. I wanted to hold the physical proof in my hands. They agreed to give me the x-ray negatives.

When the process started, the radiologist had me lay down on a cushioned platform similar to an exam table at the doctor's office. They told me I needed to stay very still, so they could get the best images possible. After I laid down on the platform, it began to move into a big machine with a round opening. I felt like I was sliding into a county morgue cadaver vault. It definitely was an eerie feeling. Soon, I began hearing a series of knocks and pings inside this giant contraption. The whole experience took just under an hour.

When the radiologist walked into the waiting room where I was anxiously waiting to hear the results of the MRI, he shook his head in disbelief with a look of shock on his face. He explained that I did indeed have agenesis of the corpus callosum. He said that not only did the scan show signs of ACC, but I learned I had complete agenesis of the corpus callosum. In other words, like Jerry, my corpus callosum is completely nonexistent.

The radiologist was in disbelief because he thought I shouldn't be able to function as well as I was with such a brain abnormality. He said he had seen ACC images before, but had never actually met anyone with ACC as severe as mine. He had assumed that a patient like myself would be more like a vegetable. He counted my situation as a miracle!

I joked with him, saying that the reason I could function as well as I have so far in life was because I'm an artist. I said, "Less is more, so since I practice this principle as an artist, it's obvious I don't need a corpus callosum!" I also joked with him, calling myself an "artistic savant."

So, how am I able to go about life on a fairly normal scale? I too consider it a wondrous miracle because my situation could have been far worse! In spite of being born with cACC, I am considered fairly high functioning. ACC is *not* a mental illness, but a neurological disorder. There is a physical difference in my brain from the average brain. While still in the womb, during the migration of brain cells, something was blocked from its normal development, causing a lack of normal callosal development. Some believe that ACC may be caused by medication taken by the mother during pregnancy.[3]

Apparently, part of my fetal brain development was organized well enough that it was able to sense the need to reorganize and restructure my brain so I could survive (though with some variables of difficulty). The results of my MRI scan showed that my brain developed Probst bundles, which are random collections of nerve fibers, gathered in abnormal areas of my brain.[4] These bundles have made up for much of what I have lost due to the lack of an actual corpus callosum.

---

3   "Pediatric Agenesis of the Corpus Callosum," *Children's National*, accessed May 5, 2017, childrensnational.org/choose-childrens/conditions-and -treatments/fetal-carepregnancy/agenesis-of-the-corpus-callosum.

4   See also Jeremy D. Schmahmann and Deepak N. Pandya, *Fiber Pathways of the Brain* (New York: Oxford University Press, 2006), 460.

In addition, during its neurological restructuring, my brain over-compensated, allowing above-average cognitive abilities in some areas—even though I am below average in other skill sets.

Many of those who suffer from ACC are far worse off than I am. ACC has a broad spectrum, which can include autism, Asperger's syndrome, and other divers neurological disorders. Many suffer from frequent brain seizures, especially those with partial agenesis—those with only part of their corpus callosum still intact. Many have additional physical or neurological impairments, with far more severe neurological and learning issues. Some cannot feed or dress themselves without help. My disability seems to have caused severe social delay, some learning delay, a sleep disorder, and some apparent mild facial malformations. There is also a possibility that my hearing impairment is connected to my cACC as well.

To manage my disability, I have had to learn to do various tasks at my own pace, which is often below average for most individuals. That's perfectly okay. In spite of my challenges, I have chosen to be proactive.

Shortly after learning that I had ACC, I signed up and qualified to participate in a clinical study for those with callosal disorders. On November 17, 2008, I flew to San Francisco and then went to the University of California—San Francisco School of Medicine, where this study took place.

While there, I underwent several tests, including MRI scans, MEG scans, CT scans, and an intensive neurological exam. For me, the neurological exam was the most valuable. The test results clearly gave me an idea of where my strengths and weaknesses fell. I was able to take this information back to two helpful therapists in Utah, who then helped me develop coping and management skills in order to handle my disability better. I considered their professional knowledge and ability to work with someone like me a great blessing. There is no known clinical treatment or medication for this disorder; there is only hard work and repetition of the things I need to learn. Gratefully, my wife and children have informed me that I am now doing considerably better.

For those who may question the experiences I've shared so far (especially the one I had when I was eight years old), and choose to attribute them to a mental illness, this intensive three-day exam would have concluded such findings. If that was the case, the therapists would have treated me for such. My disability is not a chemical imbalance. It is the result of a physical, neurological malformation of my brain.

———

In late 2010, after going through a trying time, economically and emotionally, a sliver of hope finally glimmered above the horizon. I touched base with a mural client who surprised me with three buildings that were almost ready for me to paint three new murals in. This was definitely an answer to my prayers.

During the period of time when I found little work, I spent more than the usual amount of time at the Payson City Library job hunting. Looking for something interesting to read, I came across a book titled, *Symbols In Stone: Symbolism on the Early Temples of the Restoration* by Matthew B. Brown and Paul Thomas Smith.

It was through reading this book that I discovered the fascinating world of religious symbolism. This book was an eye-opener to me as I began to discover the often subtle yet beautiful and meaningful spiritual symbolic elements found on the exteriors of religious structures, in nature, and all around me. I learned that symbolism often carries powerful layers of deeply spiritual meanings that words often do not have the power to express. As I became more aware of my new discovery, I began to see great gospel meaning emblazoned upon a variety of religious structures.

It was funny that I hadn't noticed this before. I guess God brings some things to our attention only when the time is right, and not before. The scriptures teach us that all things testify of Christ (see Moses 6:63), and I became more keenly aware of this truth. I soon found myself paying closer attention to the pair of art glass windows in the church my wife and I attend in Payson.

We moved into the LDS Payson Third Ward in July of 2008, attending the old Main Street building. Then, about eight months later, our ward moved into the new Main Street chapel, about three blocks south of the old one. But it wasn't until 2012 or 2013 that I discovered the personal significance of the pair of restored, Gothic-style art glass windows that were installed in our new chapel. God truly does manifest Himself to each of His children on a very individualized level. His divine signature to me could not have been more perfect or more personalized than the concluding story I'm about to share in the following chapter. Undeniably, God's hand was surely in it.

Chapter 14
Windows of Heaven

The Gothic-style art glass windows that were eventually placed in the Payson chapel I attended have an interesting history. The LDS Springville Second Ward chapel was built in 1904 on 451 South Main Street. It was a beautiful brick building with Gothic-style art glass windows, a wonderful pipe organ, and lots of beautiful artwork inside. After serving the LDS community for many years, it outgrew its use. This historic building was scheduled for demolition in the nineties. In spite of the scheduled demolition, the community chose to save the building because of its unique architecture.

The building was remodeled in 1998, at the cost of 1.5 million dollars, then rededicated by LDS prophet President Gordon B. Hinckley. In the fall of 1997, almost a year before the remodeling, I moved into the Springville Second Ward boundaries. It was in this beautiful building (previously mentioned in chapter 12), where I was asked to read a quote by early Elder Warren S. Snow, almost thirty-one years to the day when I had crossed the veil.

As I began to study the beautiful symbolism in the art glass windows of our Payson chapel, I asked our former bishop what he knew about the windows. I assumed that the windows were brand-new and a part of the original construction, so I was shocked when he told me where they had actually originated.

Remember

In 2006, my beloved Springville church was vandalized and set ablaze underneath the stage in the church's cultural hall. The fire made its way to the attic, until everything was engulfed in flames. The following story about the fire is from a newspaper article in the *Deseret News*:

> Police said arson was the cause of a fire that charred a historic church on Springville's Main Street late Friday night.
>
> Around 10:40 p.m., smoke billowed from the attic of a meetinghouse at 451 S. Main owned by The Church of Jesus Christ of Latter-day Saints, said Lt. Dave Caron, from the Springville department of public safety.
>
> "The fire started at the stage front (in the gym area), then got into the conduit system, which gave it access to run up the wall and into the attic," Caron said Saturday.
>
> Caron estimated that the church sustained about $200,000 worth of damage, but not all of the damage was caused by the fire. In fact, except for a broken window and a lingering smell surrounding the building, no evidence of fire could be seen from the outside.
>
> On the inside, however, the church was severely vandalized with fire extinguishers, doors were broken and televisions were smashed.[1]

As firefighters searched through the debris, they determined that the only things that could be salvaged were most of the art glass windows and possibly the pipe organ.

It was decided that the building would cost too much to be repaired and would have to be demolished. Some of the windows and the pipe organ were restored, and were installed in another LDS church building in Springville. The remaining salvaged windows were put into storage.

———

Later, another LDS church, this one on Main Street in Payson, Utah, had outgrown its use. In July 2008, Karen and I moved into this church

1 Amy Choate-Nielsen, "Arson blamed in church fire," *Deseret News*, July 30, 2006, www.deseretnews.com/article/640198632/Arson-blamed-in-church-fire.html.

building's ward boundaries. I remember attending the old church and hearing the boiler make knocking and banging noises during the sacrament service. It was always very disruptive.

A few blocks south from our new apartment, they were constructing a new church building. The construction began in 2007, almost a year before we to moved to Payson. Sometime after the new construction was underway, the LDS superintendent of construction management (over the church building project) approached our former stake president, Carl G. Swenson. This project official was also managing the construction of a new meetinghouse in Springville, Utah, replacing the beloved one that was destroyed by fire.

The project manager met President Swenson at the site where the recovered art glass windows were in storage. One pair of windows was in several separate pieces. They had been pieced together to show how they would look after installation. The offer was then made to install this pair of beautiful windows in the Payson meetinghouse currently under construction. The new building was in Payson's historic district, so the LDS official felt that the revived Gothic windows would be an appropriate addition.

President Swenson cheerfully accepted the offer, realizing that there would have to be some changes made to the standard meetinghouse construction in order for the windows to be installed. The church's steeple was also redesigned to harmonize with this unique pair of windows.

Karen and I have been attending our new church meetinghouse (the one newly constructed in Payson) since about 2009, but it wasn't until 2012 or 2013 that I discovered the personal significance of this unique pair of art glass windows. When I found out they came from my cherished fire-engulfed Springville church building, I was overcome!

When I look at this beautiful work of art, I see a symbol of the tree of life. To me, this stylized representation symbolizes my aspen tree, with the leaded breaks in the trunk representing the dark scars on a white aspen tree trunk. Think about the scars and the symbolism of the color white, and how perfectly this ties in with the love and the Light of Christ. What a great symbol for a tree of life! When the natural light of the sun shines its radiant influence through this beautiful window onto us, it adds even greater symbolic emphasis to the influence of Christ and His Atonement in our lives. It is also significant to note that stained glass was considered to be the colors of heaven during medieval times.

One of the restored art glass windows from the LDS church building in Springville, Utah. They now reside in a LDS Payson meetinghouse.

The triangular shape at the base of the tree's trunk can represent a straight path leading to the tree of life. This path, though represented in a different way, reminds me of the path in my own experience.

The triangle is also a symbol of the tree's root network. Aspen groves are not individual trees with singular root systems. An aspen grove shares a communal root network that functions as one living organism. It is a symbol of becoming one with God. This network can also symbolize our many ancestors who are laboring diligently for our benefit on the other side of the veil. Spiritually, this root network represents all of us as spiritually begotten sons and daughters of God, turning our hearts to and putting our trust in the saving power of our elder brother, Jesus Christ. Once we do this, we are then on the pathway of becoming one with Christ and our Father in Heaven.

To me, the curved shapes in the bottom corners of this window symbolize an altar of stone—specifically the altar where I stopped at the aspen tree to offer up a broken heart and a contrite spirit to God, pleading for relief from my trials. One of the two individual windows is installed right next to the sacrament table. This makes offering a broken heart and a contrite spirit even more significant, just as we are asked to do each time we partake of the sacrament.

Studying the window even further, I see lines representing a city suspended off the ground: look between the thick horizontal line at the center and the shapes just below the symbolized leaves of the tree. Here I see shapes of cathedral-like buildings or temples suspended off the ground. Can you see it? For me, this represents the city in the clouds that I saw in my experience. This is a symbol of our ultimate goal—to dwell with our Heavenly Father and His Son in the kingdom of God.

Once I recognized this symbolism, I realized that God had once again kept His promise. His handprint had been there the whole time, but I couldn't see it until my heart was ready for it. There it was again, pointing directly back to the miraculous experience I had in my youth! Now I see it each week I attend our church.

——

Like the windows, we can all be "repurposed" in the Lord's hands. He loves us and patiently takes us in our weakness. He makes us better and uses us as an instrument in His hands for a greater purpose. That purpose is to overcome this world and to ultimately become worthy to receive God's greatest gift: the gift of life eternal, dwelling with God in His kingdom.

I believe that the Savior's promise for me is His promise to all of us. No matter how alone or desperate we may feel at times in our lives, we are really not alone in this world. There is always hope, and that hope is in Christ. God loves us each individually so much that He willingly sent His Son to suffer and die for us. All He asks of us is to follow Him. We do this by obeying His commandments and loving others like the Savior did in His mortal lifetime—through loving service and ministering to their needs.

One Sunday morning (during the partaking of the sacred symbols of the sacrament), I was studying the art glass window near the sacrament table. I was reflecting on the Atonement and Christ's promised blessings I believe the Lord made me before my birth. When we partake of the bread (symbolizing the body of Christ, broken for us) and the water (symbolizing His blood), we covenant to obey His commandments and *always remember Him,* that we might have His Spirit to be with us (see D&C 20:77, 79). As I sat pondering the Savior's Atonement, I clearly felt that familiar voice of the Savior in my mind: *"Russell, as I promised, I will always remember you. Will you remember me?"* May we all do so by opening our hearts to Him.

Appendix

My Spiritual Heritage

I believe that each of us is born into this world with a royal heritage. We each have a plan and a purpose while we are here. I have come to know for myself that we are the literal spirit children of God. In other words, God first created us spiritually, before we were created physically (see Moses 3:5). I believe we existed as His spirit offspring for perhaps eons of time before we came to earth. In Jeremiah 1:5, we read, "Before I formed thee in the belly I knew thee; and before thou camest forth out of the womb I sanctified thee, *and* I ordained thee a prophet unto the nations" (italics added).

I know that God is real. He knows and loves us individually and unconditionally on a very personal level, even more so than a goodly mortal father knows and loves his own child. As a child desires and needs to feel the love and acceptance from his earthly parents, each of us can develop a similar relationship with our Heavenly Parents.

I have been blessed with a rich ancestral heritage. As a descendant of Thomas Edwin Ricks on my father's side and Edward Hunter on my mother's side, I'm very proud of my heritage. Let me tell you about these men and their descendants—my ancestors.

I was born on July 15, 1958, in Rexburg, Idaho. Rexburg was not very well known to the outside world until after the famous Teton Dam disaster that occurred on June 5, 1976. I witnessed the flood as a seventeen-year-old.

This Mormon pioneer settlement originally held the name of "Ricksburg" at its founding, in honor of my ancestor, Thomas Edwin Ricks. One day in its early history, the name was misspelled as "Rexburg" in a newspaper. ("Rex" is a German form of the surname Ricks.) Thereafter, it was forever changed to Rexburg.

When I introduce myself as, "Russell Ricks from Rexburg, Idaho," I get a chuckle from anyone familiar with Rexburg. Even LDS church members in the California mission where I served found it humorous. I guess it's like one of those tongue twisters you try saying ten times fast!

———

On November 12, 1888, shortly after the incorporation of Rexburg, Thomas Ricks established a place of learning called Bannock Academy. In 1923, this institution became Ricks College, named after its famous founder—my ancestor. Throughout the years, this institution continued to grow, spreading its influence on the world stage, until on August 10, 2001, it became BYU–Idaho.[1]

Beginning in 1846, the Mormon pioneers began migrating west,[2] moving outside the boundaries of the United States in order to escape persecution for their religious beliefs. First settling in the Salt Lake Valley, the Mormon pioneers eventually spread themselves throughout the Rocky Mountains, establishing settlements spanning from Western Canada to Mexico.[3]

---

1 "General History," *BYU–Idaho*, accessed May 5, 2017, www.byui.edu /president/past-presidents/general-history.
2 "Pioneer Trek," *Newsroom*, accessed May 5, 2017, www.mormonnewsroom org/article/pioneer-trek.
3 "The Way It Looks Today: Some LDS Settlements in the West," *Ensign*, February 1980.

Thomas Edwin Ricks was residing in Logan, Utah, and serving as the local sheriff when he received the call from his bishop to organize and establish settlements in the fertile Upper Snake River Valley.

But Thomas Ricks's story begins earlier than this.

Thomas was the oldest child of Joel Ricks and Eleanor Martin. He was born on July 21, 1828, in Trigg County, Kentucky. When he was two years old, his family moved to Madison County, Illinois. Traveling Mormon elders taught his family about the Mormon faith, and Thomas was baptized a member on February 14, 1845.

His family sold their farm in Madison County and moved to Nauvoo, Illinois[,] in September 1845. [Thomas] worked on the Nauvoo Temple from the time he arrived [in Nauvoo], until work [on the temple] was stopped and preparations commenced to move west. . . . He [crossed] westward in the Heber C. Kimball company.

When the company neared the Elkhorn River, Indians stole four of their oxen and Thomas along with three other young men were sent in pursuit. They came upon the Indians about six miles from camp. The Indians immediately [fired at the young men], and three balls entered Thomas[,] which he carried until his death. Thinking he was dead, [the other young men] left him lying on the ground and went for help. [Upon their] return, he was found to be alive and was carefully taken back to camp. He was bedridden for months.[4]

Years later, he told of a spiritual experience he had after being shot.

While I lay there weltering in blood, I thought of the condition of my father and family and how badly they needed my assistance in crossing the plains and making a home in a new land and wondered if I was going to die.

---

4   Laurel, "Thomas Edwin Ricks and Ellen Maria Yallop," *A Place to Share*, grandmalaurel.blogspot.com/2014/08/thomas-edwin-ricks-and-ellen-maria.html.

While thus engaged in thought, I heard a voice say audibly and clearly, "You will not die; you will go to the valley of the mountains and there you will do a great work in your day and generation."[5]

It was said that he was

Bold, intrepid, daring, fertile in plans and resources, with magnificent physical proportions and forceful magnetism which compelled the willing co-operation of others, he stands one of the notable figures of the pioneer days, being ever at the front whenever danger presented itself in the shape of wily foemen . . . ready to face death to protect his people from hostile attacks or the perils of starvation, when battling with the forces of elemental nature on the bleak plains of the western wilds.[6]

"A more courageous man never lived . . . for fear to him was unknown. While at times he appeared a little rough and stern in his manner and conversation . . . , beneath that sternness there always beat a kindly and forgiving heart."[7]

Thomas Ricks passed away on September 28, 1901.

—

My father's father, Henry Hans Peter Ricks, was a man of great faith. He was called to serve as a bishop in his mid-twenties, making him one of the youngest LDS bishops serving at the time.

Grandpa Ricks was born in Salem, Idaho, on January 19, 1898, to John Ricks and Julianna Fredrikke Hansen. (John was the son of Thomas Ricks.) He was born in the same town where I raised all seven of my children.

5   Marlene Bateman Sullivan, *Brigham's Boys* (Springville, Utah: CFI, 2009), 143.
6   Guy Scoby Rix, comp., *History and Genealogy of the Ricks Family of America: Containing Biographical Sketches and Genealogies of Both Males and Females* (Salt Lake City: Skelton Publishing, 1908), 104.
7   Andrew Jackson, *Latter-day Saint Biographical Encyclopedia*, vol. 1, s.v. "Ricks, Thomas Edwin," 457.

Henry Hans married Alice Elizabeth Dean. He passed away on February 21, 1963, in Rexburg, Idaho.

A few days before Grandpa passed away, he was having difficulty breathing in bed, so he moved to his overstuffed chair in order to breathe better. Grandma Alice was in the kitchen preparing food when she heard Grandpa yell, "Let me go! Alice, these little children are trying to take me!" There were no little children in the room. It was only Grandma and Grandpa at home. Could it be that angelic escorts in the form of little children came to escort Grandpa Ricks through the veil to the world of spirits?

That evening, my father wanted to visit Grandpa and invited me to go with him. I was about five years old at the time. I remember seeing Grandpa sitting up in his bed and struggling to breathe. The next day, he passed away peacefully.

Sometime after his death, my grandpa appeared to my father in a dream. He was concerned about one of Dad's brothers, who was struggling at the time. He asked Dad to keep an eye on his brother, and Dad gave him his word that he would. Before Grandpa departed, Dad asked him, "What is it like in the spirit world?" Grandpa responded with, "I'm not allowed to say, but I will tell you this much: We don't just sit around laying linoleum!" That was Grandpa's sense of humor.

———

Now I would like to introduce you to my maternal ancestor Edward Hunter. The following is a biographical sketch of Edward, penned by Orson F. Whitney, an early apostle of the Church of Jesus Christ of Latter-day Saints. This sketch was first published in the *LDS Biographical Encyclopedia*.

> [Edward Hunter], the third presiding Bishop of the Church, was the second son and seventh child of Edward and Hannah Hunter, and was born June 22, 1793, in Newton township, Delaware county, Penn. . . .

On [Edward Hunter's] mother's side, three generations back, was Robert Owen, of North Wales, a man of wealth and character, and a firm sympathizer with Cromwell and the Protectorate. On the restoration of Charles II he refused to take the oath of allegiance and was imprisoned for five years. The Bishop was fond of referring to this incident in the life of his ancestor. He would relate the circumstance in his quaint, desultory way, and coming to the close, repeat the words: "Oath of allegiance—yes, yes—refused to take it—imprisoned for five years"—and then, lifting up his hands, throwing back his head, and half shutting his eyes in a sort of dreamy ecstasy would exclaim: "Beautiful! beautiful!" . . .

After farming in Delaware county for four or five years, [Edward] removed to Chester county, where he purchased a fine farm of five hundred acres, well stocked and cultivated. He there married Ann Standly, youngest daughter of Jacob and Martha Standly, an honest, capable family of that vicinity. He was then about forty years of age.

Let the Bishop's own record now speak for him: "I always had an inquiry of the Lord as to how I could worship Him acceptably. My father told me to belong to no religious sect, but to keep sacred that all men have the right to worship God according to the dictates of their consciences. He said our form of government was too good for a wicked world, and that its blessings of liberty would not be appreciated and respected. I succeeded in business beyond my expectation. I attended different places of worship and sustained all sects in the right to worship God in their own way, but could not connect myself with any. I was called on to give the privilege to have erected on my land, on the site of an old school house which had burned down, a house for educational purposes and also for holding meetings. I agreed to give the land for ninety-nine years and help build the house, if they would allow all persons and persuasions to meet in it to worship God. This was particularly stated in the articles of agreement, and a good house was built called the West Nantmeal Seminary." . . .

Such was the state of his mind on the subject of religion, when, in the spring of 1839, he heard of a strange sect called "Mormons," some of whose preachers, traveling through that region, had learned of the

West Nantmeal Seminary and taken steps to procure the hall for the purpose of holding meetings. Immediately a tumult was raised, and it was declared by some of the leading residents that it would not do to have the "Mormons" there.

"Why?" inquired Mr. Hunter.

"Oh, they are such a terrible people," was the reply.

"Why are they terrible?" he asked.

"Why—why"—stammered the accusers—"Dr. Davis says they are a very dangerous people, and it will not do to let them preach here."

"Oh, that's it?" said the honest, independent farmer. . . . "When I gave the lease for that land and helped to build that house, it was particularly agreed and stated in the lease that people of every religion should have the privilege of meeting there to worship God. Now, those Mormons are going to have their rights, or else the lease is out and I'll take the Seminary."

This determined speech brought the bigots to their senses, and no further objection was raised. Soon after that Mr. Hunter, hearing that a "Mormon" Elder was going to preach at a place called Locust Grove, a few miles away, and that he was liable to be badly treated, mounted his horse and rode over to the meeting for the express purpose of seeing that the stranger was not imposed upon. The Elder's name was Elijah H. Davis. "He was a humble young man," says the Bishop, "the first one that I was impressed was sent of God. I was sitting by Dr. Griffith, our representative. Robert Johnson, one of the trustees, addressing the Elder, said: 'I wish you would say something about the Atonement.' He spoke well on the subject, but before he was through Johnson interrupted him and ordered him to quit preaching. I sprang up and said: 'He is a stranger and shall have justice shown him and be respected; we will hear him and then hear you speak.' I was informed that there were many present opposed to the 'Mormons,' but I resolved as I lived that Mr. Davis should be protected, if I had to meet the rabble on their own ground. I kept my eye on them and determined to stand by him at the risk of person and property. I had friends, though Mr. Davis had none. Mr. J. Johnson, brother to Robert Johnson, came to me as I was going out and apologized for his brother's conduct. I walked out of the crowd, got on my horse and rode home alone."

On reaching home and retiring for the night, he lay awake for some time meditating on what had taken place. "My reflections were," says he, "why have I taken such a decided stand for those strangers, and I asked the Lord: 'Are those Mormons thy servants?' Instantly, a light came in the room at the top of the door, so great that I could not endure it. I covered my head with the bed-clothes and turned over to the wall. I had exerted my mind and body much that day and soon fell asleep."

Mr. Hunter's house, from that time forth, was a home for all "Mormon" Elders traveling in that vicinity. During the winter of 1839–40, he was honored by a personal visit from the Prophet Joseph Smith, who was on his way back from Washington, after presenting to Pres. Van Buren the memorial of his people's grievances, and invoking, in vain, governmental protection for the Latter-day Saints, recently driven out of Missouri.

Joseph preached at the Seminary and spent several days with Mr. Hunter before proceeding westward.

[On] Oct. 8, 1840, Edward Hunter was baptized by Elder Orson Hyde, then on his way to Palestine, and soon after received a visit from Elder Hyrum Smith, the Prophet's brother. He attended conference at Philadelphia, and subscribed liberally to the building of the Nauvoo House and the Temple. At a subsequent visit of Brother Hyrum Smith, as they were walking along the banks of the Brandywine, the conversation turned upon the subject of the departed; and Brother Hunter was constrained to inquire about his children whom he had lost, particularly a little boy, George Washington by name, an excellent child to whom he was devotedly attached.

"It is pretty strong doctrine," said Elder Smith, "but I believe I will tell it. Your son will act as an angel to you; not your guardian angel, but an auxiliary angel, to assist you in extreme trials." The truth of this was manifested to him about a year and a half later, when, in an hour of deep depression, the little boy appeared to him in vision.

Brother Hunter says: "In appearance he was more perfect than in natural life—the same blue eyes, curly hair, fair complexion, and a most beautiful appearance. I felt disposed to keep him, and offered inducements for him to remain.

He then said, in his own familiar voice: [']George has many friends in heaven'."[8]

Joseph Smith once told Edward Hunter that he was related to him as a distant cousin, "I know who you are, we are near kin, I know your genealogy."[9]

———

My mother's parents, William Wallace Hunter and Bertha O'Donnell Hunter, were people of great faith. Whenever they would visit us or we would stop by for a visit, I always felt a great deal of love radiate from them. Because of this love, I grew attached to them and they became my favorite grandparents.

A few months before my Grandpa and Grandma Hunter were killed in a car accident by a drunk driver, Grandpa Hunter had a very strong impression to go purchase two grave plots—one for himself and one for his wife. On his drive back home from the cemetery, he had another impression to purchase a third plot, but didn't know why. Still, even though he thought it was strange, he obeyed the voice of the Spirit and returned to the cemetery.

About the same time, my grandparents had made friends with a widowed elderly woman, who had heard the message of the restored gospel and had been baptized a member of the Church of Jesus Christ of Latter-day Saints. After joining the LDS faith, her entire family disowned her, but she still had good friends in the LDS church, including my grandparents.

8 Andrew Jackson, *Latter-day Saint Biographical Encyclopedia*, vol. 1, s.v. "Hunter, Edward," 227–30.

9 See Vern G. Swanson, *Dynasty of the Holy Grail: Mormonism's Holy Bloodline* (Springville, Utah: CFI, 2013).

Appendix

Some time after purchasing the three grave plots and getting their affairs in order, Grandpa and Grandma Hunter paid a final visit to all of their posterity. They expressed that they felt their mission on earth was finished and that they would soon go to the other side of the veil. With their affairs now in order, it was their personal desire and their prayer to leave this world together.

Our family was the last group they paid a visit to. After saying good-bye to me, my mother, my father, and all of my siblings, they said they were leaving on a vacation to Yellowstone Park. Before their departure, they invited their new friend (the elderly widowed woman) to join them, and then they left for Yellowstone via Swan Valley.

That evening while driving the Swan Valley Pass, a drunk driver killed my grandparents and their friend instantly in a head-on collision. A few days later, all three were buried next to each other in their recently purchased plots. Sadly, their new companion's family refused to attend the funeral.

I remember the accident happening in early July 1972, a few days before my fourteenth birthday. A day or two later, I received a birthday present in the mail from my Grandpa and Grandma Hunter.

———

It is my personal witness that the veil between earth and heaven is often very thin. Those on the other side of the veil are aware of us and are concerned for our welfare. Sometimes, individuals who have passed on are given special permission to visit mortals (often their posterity) on earth, to relay messages of concern, to assist the answer to a heartfelt prayer, or to warn or bring comfort. I am proud of the trail of spiritual heritage examples that my family and ancestors have blazed for me and my posterity.

About the Author

Russell Ricks was born into a family bursting with creative energy. During his lifelong career as a visual artist, his artwork has been collected throughout the United States. From September through October 2015, Russell hung a large body of his artwork at the prestigious Springville Museum of Art as part of the Passages and Pathways exhibit. He is also well known for his monumental indoor art murals. His murals grace the walls of major corporations such as Cabela's, Novatek, and Alcoa, Inc.

Russell married Karen LaRee Samuelson on November 26, 1999. They formed a blended family with seven sons and seven daughters. Russell has four daughters and three sons, and Karen has four sons and three daughters. Russell and Karen have twenty-five grandchildren and counting.

From 1977 to 1979, Russell served a proselyting mission for The Church of Jesus Christ of Latter-day Saints in the California Oakland

and Sacramento Missions. He has also served in various callings within the LDS Church.

Russell's hobbies include hiking, horseback riding, camping, gathering reference material for future paintings, traveling to new places, and, now, writing.

Scan to visit

www.russellricksbooks.com